Charles Lamb: Man and Brother First

Charles Lamb:

Man and Brother First

David Carroll

The Book Guild Ltd

First published in Great Britain in 2024 by
The Book Guild Ltd
Unit E2 Airfield Business Park,
Harrison Road, Market Harborough,
Leicestershire. LE16 7UL
Tel: 0116 2792299
www.bookguild.co.uk
Email: info@bookguild.co.uk
X: @bookguild

Copyright © 2024 David Carroll

The right of David Carroll to be identified as the author of this work has been asserted by them in accordance with the Copyright, Design and Patents Act 1988.

All rights reserved. No part of this publication may be reproduced, transmitted, or stored in a retrieval system, in any form or by any means, without permission in writing from the publisher, nor be otherwise circulated in any form of binding or cover other than that in which it is published and without a similar condition being imposed on the subsequent purchaser.

Typeset in 11pt Minion Pro

Printed and bound by CPI Group (UK) Ltd, Croydon, CR0 4YY

ISBN 978 1835740 316

British Library Cataloguing in Publication Data.
A catalogue record for this book is available from the British Library.

For Tom McCarthy

Contents

	List of Illustrations	ix
	Acknowledgements	xi
	Foreword	xiii
Chapter One	'A Weakly but Very Pretty Babe'	1
Chapter Two	The Blue-Coat Boy	19
Chapter Three	'I Shall See Her Again in Heaven'	35
Chapter Four	'My Heart Is Quite Sunk'	54
Chapter Five	A 'Double Singleness'	70
Chapter Six	'Transplanted from Our Native Soil'	89
Chapter Seven	A Brief Romantic Interlude	111
Chapter Eight	Inter Elia	123
Chapter Nine	'From Life into Eternity'	138
Chapter Ten	'…None to Call Me Charley Now'	151
Chapter Eleven	'Worn to the Poetical Dregs'	165
	Afterword	186
	Bibliography	187
	Index of People and Places	189

List of Illustrations

1	Fountain Court, The Temple.	1
2	Mary Field's gravestone in the old churchyard at Widford.	35
3	King's Bench Walk, The Temple.	70
4	Mitre Court Buildings, The Temple.	73
5	Button Snap. (Date and source unknown.)	89
6	Bas relief medallion of Charles Lamb, on the roadside verge outside Button Snap.	109
7	Framed portrait of Charles Lamb, with signatures of founder members of the Charles Lamb Society.	112
8	Colebrooke Cottage, Islington.	125
9	Plaque on the wall of Colebrooke Cottage.	135
10	Lamb's Cottage, Church Street, Edmonton.	166
11	The gravestone of Charles and Mary Lamb in All Saints Churchyard, Edmonton.	175

Acknowledgements

Every reasonable effort has been made to trace the holders of copyright material. Any omissions are regretted, and will be rectified – upon notification – in any future edition of this work. All photographs, (with the exception of Button Snap) are from the author's own collection.

I should like to thank the following for granting permission to quote from copyright material:

Christ's Hospital Book (1953), The Society of Authors as the Literary Representative of the Estate of John Middleton Murry; extract from an article by Basil Francis in the Charles Lamb Bulletin (March 1947), Professor John Gardner, Editor of the Charles Lamb Bulletin; Visions and Revisions (G. Arnold Shaw 1915), the Estate of John Cowper Powys; Richard Holmes for Coleridge: Early Visions (Hodder & Stoughton 1989), and Coleridge: Darker Reflections (Harper Collins 1998); A Portrait of Charles Lamb by David Cecil (Constable & Co. 1983), reproduced by permission of David Higham Associates.

Foreword

Charles Lamb could best be described, perhaps, as a literary oddity. He wrote several books of stories and verse with his sister, Mary (one of which, *Tales from Shakespeare*, remains in print to this day), and others on his own. He dabbled in playwriting, but with no measurable success, and he produced copious amounts of poetry; only one example of which, *The Old Familiar Faces*, has truly endured. He produced countless articles of literary and theatrical criticism and, remarkably, all of these endeavours were undertaken during the precious hours he could spare while earning his daily bread as a clerk at the East India House in the City of London. His domestic duties and family responsibilities, too, were truly onerous and time-consuming. His name would be probably hardly known today, in fact, were it not for a long series of essays that he wrote later in his life under the pseudonym of 'Elia'. 'Pseudonym' is almost too inadequate a word to employ in this context, however, for in 'Elia' it would not be overstating the case to say that he developed an alter ego of such proportions, that for much of the time it overlapped and merged with Charles Lamb himself, making the two of them indistinguishable from one another. As a result of 'Elia', rather than becoming an all but forgotten literary name from the past, Charles Lamb is known and revered as an English

Man of Letters around the world. His name even crops up in Helene Hanff's 1970s bestseller, *84 Charing Cross Road*, and he makes a more significant contribution to Mary Ann Shaffer and Annie Barrow's epistolary novel of 2008, *The Guernsey Literary and Potato Peel Pie Society*, wherein he unwittingly helps bring together two lovers in the aftermath of the Second World War.

During the early days of researching this short biography, my eye was caught by an article in the March 1947 issue of the *Charles Lamb Bulletin*, the organ (as it was quaintly described in those far-off days) of the Charles Lamb Society. Written by Basil Francis, who had recently published a biography of the noted actress Fanny Kelly (who became a friend of Charles Lamb), it provided a cautionary note for the task which lay ahead of me. "Of all forms of literary endeavour," he wrote, "biography is at once the most fascinating and the most tantalising. At best it is possible to reach only an approximation to the true story of a 'life'… There are so many unchronicled gaps, and so many 'faithful records' which the unwary author may be tempted to quote as authoritative when they speak with no more authority than an imperfect memory aided by a lively imagination can devise." In short, as a biographer you must always check and treble check your sources. This principle I have attempted to follow to the letter.

Chapter One

'A Weakly but Very Pretty Babe'

Fountain Court, The Temple

Sauntering through the squares and courtyards, and among the immaculately tended gardens and rows of barristers' chambers that largely comprise the Temple, sandwiched between London's Victoria Embankment to the south and Fleet Street to the north, it is not difficult to imagine the ghost of

Charles Lamb toddling along behind you. (One friend of his adult years described his gait as "advancing with a motion from side to side, between involuntary consciousness and attempted ease".) His spectral presence would hardly be surprising, because he seemed at various times of his life attached to the Temple as if by an umbilical cord. The image is an apt one. He was born in the Temple, and it remained his family's home for the first seventeen years of his life. Later, he would return to spend sixteen of his adult years there, too. Residing in the Temple seemed always to provide the benchmark for him against which he measured living anywhere else. Its precincts had burrowed deep into his soul. Charles described the Temple, in fact, as "the most elegant spot in the metropolis… What a transition for the countryman visiting London for the first time – the passing from the crowded Strand or Fleet Street, by unexpected avenues, into its magnificent ample squares, its classical green recesses". The American writer, Washington Irving, concurred on entering the chapel of the Knights Templars. "I do not know a more impressive lesson for the man of the world," he wrote, "than thus suddenly to turn aside from the high way of busy money seeking life and sit down among these shadowy sepulchres, where all is twilight, dust and forgetfulness."

In his peerless *London: The Biography* (2000), our greatest modern chronicler of the capital, Peter Ackroyd, wrote of the "three hundred year-old fountain to be found amid the buildings of the Temple, commemorated by writers as diverse as Dickens and Verlaine, while the softness and serenity of this small spot [Fountain Court] have been experienced by many generations". It was in his novel *Martin Chuzzlewit* that Dickens immortalised the fountain in a scene where two of his characters, John Westlock and Ruth Pinch meet. "Brilliantly the Temple fountain sparkled in the sun, and laughingly its liquid music played, and merrily the idle drops of water danced and danced, and, peeping out in sport among the trees, plunged lightly down to hide themselves, as little Ruth and her companion came towards it." The fountain exerts its charm to the present day; the very same fountain that Charles loved as a child. "Which I have made to rise and fall, how many times, to the astoundment of the young urchins, my contemporaries, who, not being able to guess at its recondite machinery, were almost tempted to hail the wondrous work as magic!"

Ackroyd himself first visited the Temple as a schoolboy, as he explained in his biography of London, "with no knowledge of its history or its associations, and immediately fell under the spell of its enchantment; it was as if innumerable good acts or kind words had emerged here as calmly and as quietly as the little fountain itself. At last, in these pages, he has the chance of recording his debt".

***

The Temple comprises the Inner and Middle Temple, two of the historic Inns of Court (professional associations for barristers in England and Wales). The remaining two are Gray's Inn and Lincoln's Inn. Inner Temple and Middle Temple have occupied the site of buildings once belonging to the crusading Order of Knights Templars (or Red Cross Knights) since the fourteenth century. Middle Temple Hall was reputedly the setting for the first performance of Shakespeare's *Twelfth Night* during the Christmas period of 1601. "That Shakespeare on this occasion took an active part is not improbable, since he was then a member of the Globe company, which alone was capable of producing his plays," wrote Hugh H.L. Bellot in *The Inner and Middle Temple: Legal, Literary and Historic Associations* (1902). "In any case, he may well have been present. And here, too, Elizabeth must have come, accompanied by her Court, to witness the play, or to lead the dance with Christopher Hatton [later to be appointed her Lord Chancellor] or some equally comely courtier. We can well picture the Virgin Queen in this stately hall, the centre of a brilliant group of statesmen and lawyers, soldiers and sailors, poets and courtiers."

It was into this sequestered environment that Charles Lamb was born, at 2 Crown Office Row, on the 10th of February 1775. He was christened exactly a month later, on the 10th of March, at the nearby Temple Church. There were two godfathers in attendance; one was a gunsmith whose name was Henshaw, but all other details about him are lost in the mists of time. The other was Francis Fielde, described as an oilman of Holborn. Charles would later write of him that he "was the most gentlemanly of oilmen, grandiloquent yet courteous".

The 10th of February was, by chance, a fitting date for Charles's nativity. Hardly to be described as a cautious drinker throughout his life (except for those infrequent interludes when he made a gallant effort to abstain from alcohol), the day has an association – albeit a tragic one – with intoxicating liquor. It marked the anniversary of the start of a riot which broke out at the Swindlestock Tavern in Oxford in 1355. A group of students from the university were celebrating the feast day of the sixth-century Catholic nun, St. Scholastica. As the hours wore on, and the drink took its inevitable toll, a few of the students complained to the landlord about the quality of his ale and wine. This was obviously a bad move and a heated dispute erupted, which quickly spilled out on to the surrounding streets. The number of combatants swelled alarmingly, as news of the riot spread through Oxford. As a result, 'town and gown' were at each other's throats for a full three days. Nearly one hundred people, students and townsfolk, died in the melee.

The building where Charles was born looked out – as it still does today in its rebuilt form – over Temple Gardens, towards the Embankment and the River Thames beyond. Crown Office Row was built in 1737, replacing an earlier warren of chambers that had itself been reconstructed in 1628. Thus the site has a long and distinguished history. In common with large swathes of the City of London, the Temple sustained a great deal of bomb damage during the Second World War, and Crown Office Row was one of the buildings badly affected by enemy action. Subsequently, much restoration work has been carried out, reclaiming wherever possible the original material to help preserve the historical character of the area.

The Temple has been the haunt of many literary men over the centuries. The seventeenth-century diarist John Evelyn, for example, lived in Essex Court (off Fountain Court) in 1640, and Oliver Goldsmith, author of *The Deserted Village* (1770), occupied chambers on the second floor of 2 Brick Court in 1765, "but a biscuit toss from Crown Office Row", as B.E. Martin observed in *In the Footprints of Charles Lamb* (1891). "Perhaps little Mary Lamb sometimes met, within the grounds, the short, stout, plain, pock-marked Irish doctor." He died in those chambers only ten months before Charles was born. "Here, as in the day of Edmund Spenser," added Martin, "on every hand we see the shades of William Congreve, William Cowper, Henry Fielding, Dr. Johnson and James Boswell." It is no wonder that, having been brought up in such a literary atmosphere, Charles turned out to be a writer. In more recent times, the Temple's historic buildings, cobbled streets and atmospheric period lighting have become a familiar sight to millions of people throughout the world, most of whom will never have set foot near the Temple in their lives. The reason is that it has become an immensely popular location for production companies making period films and television dramas.

***

Charles Lamb: Man and Brother First

Charles was the youngest of the three surviving Lamb children by quite some margin. (Four other offspring, two girls and two boys had died during infancy before he was born.) His sister, Mary Anne, but always known simply as Mary, and the closest of the siblings to him in age, was just over ten years his senior, and almost like a second mother to him during his infancy and childhood. His brother, John, had been born eighteen months before Mary. Their father, also named John, was born in 1738 and was just under forty when Charles appeared. He had left his native Lincolnshire as a young lad and gone into service in London. There are just a few tantalising scraps of information to be gleaned relating to the history of the Lamb family prior to John's arrival in London. It seems likely that he was a native of Stamford, and later moved to Lincoln. E.V. Lucas, in his exhaustive *A Life of Charles Lamb* (2 vols. 1905), refers to a tongue-in-cheek list of "titles of honour" which Charles compiled when writing to a friend in 1810, in which he finally opted for 'Baron Lamb of Stamford', "where my family came from".

At the time of his youngest son's birth, John Lamb was employed as an assistant and servant to the distinctively named Samuel Salt, a Bencher of the Inner Temple, and the Lamb family was accommodated in one of his two sets of chambers. (A Bencher is a senior member of an Inn of Court, and thus Salt was a person of some consequence.) The relationship between John Lamb and his employer seems to have been decidedly more companionable than the term 'master and servant' would ordinarily suggest in late-eighteenth century England. In fact, Salt turned out to be not only John Lamb's employer, but also a generous benefactor to him and his family. During Salt's lifetime, the Lambs enjoyed relative comfort and freedom from the worst of financial cares, and indeed from many of those everyday tribulations that a family placed in their humble circumstances might normally expect to encounter. There is a pleasing vignette of John Lamb as he appeared in his prime, rendered by Charles in lines he wrote about his father in 1798:

> ...a merrier man
> A man more apt to frame matter for mirth,
> Mad jokes, and antics for a Christmas eve,
> Making life social, and the laggard time
> To move on nimbly, never yet did cheer
> The little circle of domestic friends.

However, Charles painted a more rounded portrait of his father in an essay entitled *The Old Benchers of the Inner Temple*, which was written and published in 1820. It was one of the pieces he wrote during the latter part of his life under the pseudonym 'Elia', of whom we shall hear a great deal in future chapters. In *The Old Benchers...* the reader could easily be duped into believing that the essay contains unvarnished biography. However, writing as his alter ego, Charles urges caution: "Let no one receive the narratives of Elia for true records. They are, in truth, but shadows of fact, – verisimilitudes, not verities...".

It is in this spirit that the reader must always remember to approach them. Thus, John Lamb appears in the essay as 'Lovel'. He was, explained Elia, Salt's "clerk, his good servant, his dresser, his friend... his guide, stop-watch, auditor, treasurer. He did nothing without consulting Lovel or failed in anything without expecting and fearing his admonishing. He put himself almost too much in his hands, had they not been the purest in the world. He resigned his title almost to respect as a master, if L. could ever have forgotten for a moment that he was a servant".

Lovel was, in fact, a man of many parts, and "of an incorrigible and losing honesty. A good fellow withal [who] took a hand at quadrille or bowls with equal facility; made punch better than any man of his degree in England; had the merriest quips and conceits, and was altogether as brimful of rogueries and inventions as you could desire. He was a brother of the angle, moreover, and just such a free, hearty, honest companion as Mr. Izaak Walton would have chosen to go a-fishing with. I saw him in his old age [when] at intervals… he would speak of his former life, and how he came up a little boy from Lincoln to go to service, and how his mother cried at parting with him, and how he returned, after some few years absence, in his smart new livery, to see her, and she blessed herself at the change, and could hardly be brought to believe that it was 'her own bairn'."

The same essay introduced the reader to an Elian version of Salt himself. "Salt had the reputation of being a very clever man, and of excellent discernment in the chamber practice of the law. I suspect his knowledge did not amount to much. When a case of difficult disposition of money, testamentary or otherwise, came before him, he ordinarily handed it over with a few instructions to his man Lovel, who was a quick little fellow, and would despatch it out of hand by the light of natural understanding, of which he had an uncommon share. It was incredible what repute for talents S. enjoyed by the mere trick of gravity… [He] was thought by some of the greatest men of his time a fit person to be consulted, not alone in matters pertaining to the law, but in the ordinary niceties and embarrassments of conduct – from the force of manner entirely."

***

While little is known about the Lincolnshire roots of John Lamb's family, a considerable amount of interesting detail has been unearthed regarding Charles's mother, Elizabeth Lamb, whose own history was steeped in the soil of what her younger son described as "hearty, homely loving Hertfordshire". She was born in Hitchin where her own mother, Mary Bruton, had married a gardener named Edward Field in September 1736. The couple were both from well-established local families, but little is known about their subsequent marriage. Mary Field's sister, Ann, married – at King's Walden – a Hertfordshire farmer named James Gladman, of Mackery End, in May 1747. He was described as a "substantial yeoman" and was the scion of another well-known local family. When Charles was a young boy, and Mary in her early teens, together they had visited their Great-Aunt Ann at Mackery End. "…or Mackarel End, as it is spelt, perhaps more properly in some old maps of Hertfordshire, a farmhouse delightfully situated within a gentle walk from Wheathampstead," as Charles described it in his Elia essay, *Mackery End in Hertfordshire* (1821). "The oldest thing I remember is Mackery End," he wrote. "I can just remember having been there, on a visit to a great-aunt, when I was a child…" Mary took him on this visit in 1779, when he was four. The timber-framed building dated from at least the early seventeenth century. (To avoid confusion for anyone visiting the area today, it should be noted that Mackery End is also the name of the mansion where – in Charles's day – the gentry lived. Elia's Mackery End was the nearby farmhouse.)

Mary Field, Charles's maternal grandmother, was also still living in Hertfordshire when he was growing up. At some point during the 1740s, she had entered the employ of the Plumer family, whose wealth can be traced back to the reign of Elizabeth I. Mrs. Field was appointed as the caretaker (a position she would occupy for almost half a century) of Blakesware, the Plumer family home near Widford dating from the 1640s. It was described in one account as "an ancient mansion, topped by many turrets, gables, carved chimneys, guarded all about by a solid red-brick wall and heavy iron gates".

Charles wrote about his childhood memories of Blakesware in his Elia essay, *Blakesmoor in H—Shire* (1824), with its marble busts of Roman Caesars in the hall, and Hogarth prints on the walls; all of which made a great impression on his young mind. "I do not know a pleasure more affecting," he wrote in the years of his maturity, "than to range at will over the deserted apartments of some fine old family mansion. The traces of extinct grandeur admit of a better passion than envy; and contemplations on the great and good, whom we fancy in succession to have been its inhabitants, weave for us illusions, incompatible with the bustle of modern occupancy, and vanities of foolish present aristocracy… Every plank and panel of that house for me had magic in it. I was a lonely child, and had the range at will of every apartment, knew every nook and corner, wondered and worshipped everywhere… In the cheerful storeroom I used to sit and read [the seventeenth-century poet Abraham] Crowley, and the hum and flappings of that one solitary wasp that ever haunted it about me – it is in mine ears now, as oft as summer returns."

In October 1799, after revisiting the area around Blakesware as a young man (although Mary Field had died in 1792, "bowed down with cancer"), Charles wrote to his friend, the poet Robert Southey, "[I have just] returned from Herts, where I have passed a few red-letter days with much pleasure. I would describe the county to you, as you have done by Devonshire; but alas! I am a poor pen at that same. I could tell you of an old house with a tapestry bedroom, the 'Judgement of Solomon' composing [sic] one panel… I could tell of a wilderness and of a village church, and where the bones of my honoured grandam lie; but there are feelings which refuse to be translated."

***

'A Weakly but Very Pretty Babe'

Following the death in 1767 of William Plumer, at the age of eighty, Mary Field was retained by his son to act as housekeeper and companion to his elderly and newly widowed mother. When old Mrs. Plumer eventually died in 1778, Charles's grandmother stayed on at Blakesware where, for most of the time, she lived in the mansion entirely alone, and would continue to do so until her own death fourteen years later. "Though indeed she was not the mistress [of Blakesware], but had only the charge of it," wrote Charles, "she still lived in it in a manner as if it had been her own, and kept up the dignity of the great house in a sort while she lived."

Mary Field was laid to rest in the old churchyard at Widford, in the shadow of Blakesware, "and in the consecrated plot of her grandson's heart", as Reginald Hine observed in *Charles Lamb and His Hertfordshire* (1949). Although Charles had dearly loved his old grandmother, she could appear a somewhat daunting figure to a young child, as he wrote in the *Gem* in 1830. "The tender mercies of the wicked are cruel. I am always disposed to add, so are those of Grandmothers. Mine had never failing pretexts of tormenting children for their own good… I well remember when a fly had got into a corner of my eye, and I was complaining of it to her, the old lady deliberately pounded two ounces or more of the finest loaf sugar that could be got, and making me hold open the eye as wide as I could – all innocent of her purpose – she blew from delicate white paper, with a full breath, the whole saccharine contents into the part afflicted, saying, 'There, now the fly is out!' 'Twas most true – a legion of blue-bottles, with the prince of flies at their head, must have dislodged with the torrent and deluge of tears which followed… Her medicine-case was a perfect magazine of tortures for infants. She seemed to have no notion of the comparatively tender drenches which young internals require – her potions were anything but milk for babes… But of all her nostrums – rest her soul – nothing came up to the Saturday night's flannel – that rude fragment of a Witney blanket... thrust into the corners of a weak child's eye, with soap that might have whitened the hands of Duncan's She-murderer, and scowered [sic] away Original Sin itself."

***

The courtship and subsequent marriage of Charles and Mary's parents is almost certainly explained by the fact that Salt was a member of the Plumer family's circle of friends. When Salt visited Blakesware from time to time, his servant-cum-assistant would have inevitably travelled into Hertfordshire with him where, at some point in the proceedings, John Lamb and the housekeeper's daughter, Elizabeth Field, obviously met in the daily hectic round of life 'below stairs'. Their wedding took place in London, at St. Dunstan's-in-the-Field, on the 29th of March 1761.

It was said of Elizabeth Lamb that, physically, she resembled the celebrated actress of the day, Mrs. Siddons, to the extent that they might almost be mistaken for sisters. Meanwhile, her husband, by all accounts, bore a definite resemblance to the great actor-manager, David Garrick. However, a more tangible theatrical connection was supplied by Charles's godfather, Fielde, who was, according to his godson, "a tall grave person, lofty in speech, and had pretensions above his rank. He associated with John Palmer, the comedian. He was also known to and visited by [Richard Brinsley] Sheridan... From either of these connexions [sic], it may be inferred that my godfather could command an order [i.e. free tickets] for the then Drury-lane theatre at pleasure – and, indeed, a pretty liberal issue of those cheap billets, in Brinsley's easy autograph, I have heard him say was the sole remuneration which he had received for many years' nightly illumination of the orchestra...".

Notwithstanding the fact that Lucas, Charles's biographer, was unable to confirm the connection with Sheridan, we learn from Charles's own pen that it was his godfather Fielde who provided the tickets for him to see his first play on the 1st of December 1780, when he was a mere five years of age. The programme for the evening comprised Thomas Arne's opera, *Artaxerxes* (quite a taxing experience for such a young child, one could well imagine), followed by a pantomime, *Harlequin's Invasion*. Charles held dear the memory of his first visit to a theatre throughout his life, as his Elia essay on the subject attests. "At the north end of Cross Court," he wrote, "there yet stands a portal, of some architectural pretensions, though reduced to humble use, serving at present [1821] for an entrance to a printing-office. This old doorway, if you are young, reader, you may not know was the identical pit entrance to old Drury – Garrick's Drury – all of it that is left. I never pass it without shaking some forty years off my shoulders, recurring to the evening when I passed through it to see MY FIRST PLAY! The afternoon had been wet, and the condition of our going… was, that the rain should cease. With what a beating heart did I watch from the window the puddles, from the stillness of which I was taught to prognosticate the desired cessation! I seem to remember the last spurt, and the glee with which I ran to announce it… The next play to which I was taken was the *Lady of the Manor*, of which, with the exception of some scenery, very faint traces are left in my memory… My third play followed in quick succession. It was the *Way of the World*. I think I must have sat at it as grave as a judge: for, I remember, the hysteric affectations of good Lady Wishfort affected me like some solemn tragic passion… I saw these plays in the season 1781–2, when I was from six to seven years old. After the intervention of six or seven other years (for at school all playgoing was inhibited) I again entered the doors of a theatre."

It was inevitable that Charles would become a lifelong devotee of the theatre after those early experiences (he described it as "the most delightful of recreations"), and in the fulness of time, perhaps, fall boyishly in love with a famous Drury Lane actress who, sadly, could not return his love. Charles would write four plays during the course of his life, but none of them would prove to be a success. Three of the plays – Elizabethan-style tragedies – were never acted, and the fourth, *Mr. H.-*, a farce produced at Drury Lane in 1806, was hissed off the stage on its first night. He was to prove much more successful, however, when writing about the theatre, and he eventually became a highly respected critic.

***

As an infant and young boy growing up in Salt's chambers, Mary was always Charles's closest companion. Their elder brother, John, already twelve-years-old when Charles was born, and undoubtedly his mother's favourite child, never formed a part of the tight bond which bound Charles and Mary together, and which continued unbroken for fifty-nine years, until the day Charles died. Given the disparity in their ages, it was perhaps inevitable that the two brothers would never become really close to each other; after all, Charles was barely of school age when John first went out to work. Apart from the usual family ties they had little in common; not least their personalities, which were unalike from the beginning and continued to develop along very different lines as they grew up. Gentleness, kindness, a generous and forgiving nature laced with a love of good fellowship, were some of the characteristics that defined Charles throughout his life; while a thumbnail sketch of John (a simplification, admittedly) might well depict him as self-centred and rude. It was entirely typical of Charles that, after John's death in 1821, he should present the reader with another version of his brother in his Elia essay, *Dream Children: A Reverie*

(1822): "So handsome and spirited a youth, a king to the rest of us; and, instead of moping about in solitary corners, like some of us, he would mount the most mettlesome horse he could get, when but an imp… and make it carry him half over the county in a morning, and join the hunters when they were out…".

In doing so, Charles was describing a protective and valiant elder brother of his imagination, rather than the hero who was denied to him in real life. "When he died, though he had not been dead an hour, it seemed as if he had died a great while ago, such a distance there is betwixt life and death; and how I bore his death as I thought pretty well at first, but afterwards it haunted and haunted me; and though I did not cry or take it to heart as some do, and as I think he would have done if I had died, yet I missed him all day long, and knew not till then how much I had loved him. I missed his kindness and I missed his crossness, and wished him to be alive again, to be quarrelling with him (for we quarrelled sometimes), rather than not have him again…".

***

Eleven years of age when her youngest brother was born, Mary doted from the outset on the infant Charles, and within a handful of years had firmly established herself as his surrogate mother. Whereas John, the Lambs' eldest child, was his mother's 'blue-eyed boy', Charles believed (as he related in a letter written to his friend Samuel Taylor Coleridge in 1796) that "…my mother never understood Mary right. She loved her as she loved us all, with a Mother's love; but [she] bore so distant a resemblance to her daughter, that she could never understand her right… and met [Mary's] caresses, and protestations of filial affection, too frequently with coldness and repulse… Yet she would always love my brother above Mary, who was not worthy of one tenth of that affection, which Mary had a right to claim".

In addition to both parents and their three children, one other person shared the family hearth at 2 Crown Office Row. It may be imagined, therefore, that living conditions were somewhat cramped, and could even become a little oppressive at times. Sarah Lamb, known within the family as Aunt Hetty, was John Lamb Senior's unmarried sister. It was not always the case that a state of perfect amity existed between Elizabeth Lamb and her sister-in-law. "They were, in their different ways, the best creatures in the world – but they set out wrong at first," Mary recalled. "They made each other miserable for full twenty years of their lives – my Mother was a perfect gentlewoman, my Aunt as unlike a gentlewoman as you can possibly imagine a good old woman to be; so that my dear Mother... used to distress and weary her with incessant and unceasing attention. The old woman could not return this in kind, and did not know what to make of it – thought it all deceit, and used to hate my mother with a bitter hatred; which, of course, was soon returned with interest." Young Charles, however, adored his Aunt Hetty, and she returned his love in full. "I had an aunt," he wrote in his Elia essay, *My Relations* (1821), "a dear and good one. She was one whom single blessedness had soured to the world. She often used to say that I was the only thing in it which she loved; and when I thought I was quitting it, she grieved over me with mother's tears. She was from morning till night poring over good books and devotional exercises. Her favourite volumes were Thomas a Kempis... and a Roman Catholic Prayer Book... She persisted in reading them, although admonished daily concerning their Papistical tendency... She was a woman of strong sense, and a shrewd mind – extraordinary at repartee; one of the few occasions of her breaking silence – else she did not much value wit. The only secular employment I remember to have seen her engaged in was the splitting of French beans, and dropping them into a china basin of fair water. The odour of those tender vegetables to this day comes back upon my senses, redolent of soothing recollections."

When Charles was five Mary was in her mid-teens (although the concept of the teenager hadn't been invented then!) and she devoted much of her time to teaching and amusing her young brother. Mary had a good heart and a gentle nature, and "…with a childish wisdom born, surely, not of her years, but rather of her loneliness and her unrequited caresses, and her craving for companionship, she became at once his big sister, his little mother, his guardian angel", wrote Martin. "She cared for him in his helpless babyhood, she gave strength to his feeble frame, she nurtured his growing brain, she taught him to talk and to walk." In her old age, Mary recalled the infant Charles as a "weakly but very pretty babe". Perhaps she had in mind the time when, at the age of five, he was struck down with smallpox, a malady that so often proved fatal in the late-eighteenth century. On another occasion, Charles became so lame that he had to be carried around by his sturdy brother John. He recalled, somewhat regretfully, in *Dream Children A Reverie*, how John "used to carry me upon his back when I was a lame-footed boy – for he was a good bit older than me – many a mile when I could not walk for pain; and how in after life he became lame-footed too, and I did not always (I fear) make allowances enough for him when he was impatient or in pain, nor remember sufficiently how considerate he had been to me when I was lame-footed…". In fact, John's condition was a very serious one. In 1796 he was involved in an accident, in which a large stone was blown down on to his foot during a high wind. The surgeon treating him had considered amputation, but the limb was eventually saved.

***

Charles was, by his own admission, an abnormally nervous child. Perhaps he simply possessed an over-active imagination, but there was a degree of mental instability in his family, and in due season he was to inherit his small share of it. Perhaps his infant terrors were a harbinger of this. "The night-time solitude and the dark were my hell," he explained, in his Elia essay on *Witches and other Night-fears* (1821). "The sufferings I endured in this nature would justify the expression. I never laid my head on my pillow, I suppose, from the fourth to the seventh or eighth year of my life – so far as memory serves in things so long ago – without an assurance, which realised its own prophecy, of seeing some frightful spectre… I durst not, even in the daylight, once enter the chamber where I slept, without my face turned to the window, aversely from the bed where my witch-ridden pillow was. Parents do not know what they do when they leave tender babes alone to go to sleep in the dark. The feeling about for a friendly arm – the hoping for a familiar voice – when they wake screaming – and find none to soothe them. What a terrible shaking it is to their poor nerves! The keeping them up till midnight, through candlelight and the unwholesome hours, as they are called, – would, I am satisfied, in a medical point of view, prove the better caution."

On a happier note, it was in Salt's chambers that Charles, accompanied by Mary, first "tumbled", as he expressed it, "into a spacious closet of good old English reading, and browsed at will on that fair and wholesome pasturage". In allowing Charles and his sister the run of his large and eclectic library at such an early age, the family's trusty old benefactor helped both to foster and nourish their love of literature; a mutual pleasure that would later serve them well when they embarked upon their joint literary enterprises. More importantly, perhaps, it would help to sustain them throughout their lives, in the good times and the bad.

Chapter Two

The Blue-Coat Boy

Charles's formal education began under the kindly and elementary tuition of a Mrs. Reynolds, whose father had resided in the Temple. She had married unhappily and lived apart from her husband. At best, the nature of the education that Charles received at her hands would have been only of the most basic kind (Charles was barely five at this time); no doubt she taught him the alphabet and simple numbers. Even this may not have been strictly necessary, however, as he had learned to read at a very tender age under Mary's guidance and, writes Lucas, "he knew his letters before he could talk".

The poet and journalist, Thomas Hood, who would later become a good friend of Charles and, at one stage, his neighbour, has left a vivid portrait of Mrs. Reynolds in her seventies, drawn by observing her at various social gatherings hosted by the Lambs in their later years, when living at Islington and Enfield. This suggests, of course, that Charles stayed in touch with his earliest schoolteacher throughout her long life. She was, wrote Hood, in his comic miscellany, *Hood's Own*, "...an elderly lady, formal, fair and flaxen-wigged, looking remarkably like a flaxen-haired doll. When she spoke, it was as if by an artificial apparatus, and she had a slight limp and a twist in her figure... This antiquated personage had been Lamb's schoolmistress, and on this retrospective consideration, though she could hardly have taught him more than to read his native tongue – he allowed her in her decline a yearly sum equal to – what shall I say? – to the stipend which some persons of fortune deem sufficient for the active services of an all-accomplished gentlewoman in the education of their children, say, thirty pounds per annum". This was striking generosity indeed from a man who, although never exactly poverty-stricken, could at no stage in his life have been described as truly well off.

It was in 1780 that Charles found himself in the gentle care of Mrs. Reynolds. At such a young age, it is inconceivable that he was aware of the momentous events being played out close to his home in the Temple at the beginning of June in that year. Spearheaded by Lord George Gordon, Chief of the Protestant Association, and after whom the riots were duly named, tens of thousands of anti-Catholic demonstrators, protesting against the relaxation of discrimination against Catholics living in Britain (as laid out in the Papists Act of 1778), marched on the Houses of Parliament. Scores of buildings were attacked and looted in the process, including Newgate Prison. Order was eventually restored by the army, but the riots lasted throughout the first week of June. It was estimated that up to seven hundred people lost their lives. Dr. Johnson's biographer, James Boswell, described the riots as "the most horrid series of outrage that ever disgraced a civilized country".

***

Although details of Charles's life are sparse for this period, it was probably in the autumn of 1780, a few months after the rioting had been quelled, that he left behind Mrs. Reynolds's cosy little schoolroom, and entered the academy belonging to a Mr. William Bird, whose dingy premises were situated off Fetter Lane, a mere stone's throw north of the Temple. To describe Mr. Bird's establishment as an 'academy' is probably akin to a bricklayer calling himself a stonemason. Bird styled himself a 'Teacher of Mathematics and Languages', according to the inscription painted above his schoolroom door, but "Heaven knows what languages were taught in it then", Charles reflected almost half-a-century later, in William Hone's *Every Day Book*. "I am sure that neither my sister nor myself brought any out of it, but a little of our native English." (Bird's was a co-educational establishment: boys were taught in the morning and girls in the afternoon.) "I well remember Bird," Charles continued. "He was a squat, corpulent middle-sized man, with something of the gentleman about him, and that peculiar mild tone – especially when he was inflicting punishment – which is so much more terrible to children, than the angriest looks and gestures. Whippings were not frequent; but when they took place, the correction was performed in a private room adjoining, whence we could only hear the plaints, but saw nothing. This heightened the decorum and the solemnity. But the ordinary public chastisement was the bastinado, a stroke or two on the palm with that almost obsolete weapon now – the ferule. I have an intense recollection of that disused instrument of torture and the malignancy, in proportion to the apparent mildness, with which its strokes were applied… By no process can I look back upon this blister-raiser with anything but unmingled horror. To make him look more formidable – if a pedagogue had need of these heightenings – Bird wore one of those flowered Indian gowns, formerly in use with schoolmasters; the strange figures upon which we used to interpret into hieroglyphics of pain and suffering. But boyish fears apart, Bird was I believe in the main a humane and judicious master. O, how I remember our legs wedged into those uncomfortable sloping desks, where we sat elbowing each other… the truant looks side-long to the garden, which seemed a mockery of our imprisonment… our little leaden inkstands, not separately subsisting, but sunk into the desks; the bright, punctually washed morning fingers, darkening gradually with another and another ink-spot. What a world of little associated circumstances, pains and pleasures mingling their quotas of pleasure, arise at the reading of those few simple words – 'Mr. William Bird, an eminent Writer, and Teacher of languages and mathematics in Fetter Lane, Holborn!'"

Mary, too, had been a pupil of Bird's before Charles arrived at the academy. But as a girl brought up in her time and circumstances, this no doubt comprised the extent of her formal education. For Charles, on the other hand, a rigorous academic career lay ahead.

***

By October 1782, Charles had left Bird's Academy behind him and, on the ninth of that month, entered on his career at Christ's Hospital, widely referred to as the 'Blue-Coat School', owing to its traditional Tudor uniform of a belted long blue coat, knee-breeches and yellow socks. At the time, he was a few months short of his eighth birthday. The origins of the foundation of Christ's Hospital lay in Henry VIII's infamous policy to dissolve the monasteries. One victim of that Act of 1535 was the thirteenth-century Convent of the Grey Friars, which stood in the parish of St. Nicholas in the Shambles near Newgate. These were the buildings that, from 1552, were occupied by the pupils and teachers of Christ's Hospital. The essayist, poet and editor, James Leigh Hunt, the son of a poor clergyman, entered Christ's Hospital in 1791, only two years after Charles had quit. He has left a detailed description, in his *Autobiography* (1850), of the school that greeted him on his arrival, and which in that form is now long gone. "There is a quadrangle with cloisters," he explained, "and the square inside the cloisters is called the Garden, and most likely was the monastery garden. Its only delicious crop for many years, has been pavement. Another large area, presenting the Grammar and Navigation Schools, is also misnomered the Ditch; the town ditch having formerly run that way. In Newgate Street is seen the Hall, or eating room, one of the noblest in England, adorned with enormously long paintings by Verrio and others, and with an organ. A portion of the old quadrangle once contained the library of the monks, and was built or repaired by the famous Whittington, whose arms were to be seen outside… The wards, or sleeping rooms, are twelve, and contained in my time two rows of beds on each side, partitioned off, but connected with one another, and each having two boys to sleep in it. Down the middle ran the binns for holding bread and other things, and serving for a table when the meal was not taken in the hall; and over the binns hung a great homely chandelier. To each of these wards a nurse was assigned, who was the widow of some decent liveryman of London, and who had the charge of looking after us at night-time, seeing to our washing etc., and carving for us at dinner: all of which gave her a good deal of power, more than her name warranted."

Christ's Hospital comprised five schools: a mathematical (or navigation) school whose pupils, Leigh Hunt explained, went as midshipmen into the naval and East India Service; the writing school, intended for those boys who went into trade and commerce; the grammar school, whose pupils (of which Charles was one) went mainly into the Church or to university; the reading school, on the other hand, catered for pupils who could not read when they entered Christ's Hospital; and, finally, the drawing school. "There were few in [it], and I scarcely know what they did, or for what object," he remarked tartly. This, then, was Christ's Hospital, exactly as Charles would have known it.

Latterly styled a coeducational independent day and boarding school, Christ's Hospital has been a charity school from the beginning. Its continuing aim is the provision of places to pupils from all backgrounds who show academic potential, but who might otherwise – for whatever reason – find themselves denied entry to a public school education.

Christ's Hospital, during the years when Charles was a pupil, was situated on a large area of ground bordered by St. Bartholomew's Hospital, Newgate Street, Little Britain and Giltspur Street, just a brisk walk from the Temple. From 1707, girls were catered for at a separate site in Hertford where, from 1761, some of the junior boys aged under ten were also accommodated. In 1902 the school moved out of London, and established itself at Horsham in West Sussex, where it continues to flourish up to the present day. However, there were initially some doubts about the wisdom of the move. An article in *The Times* claimed that "by the proposed migration from London so much of the old character of the school must be destroyed that it would perhaps be an anachronism to preserve the rest; and we must probably reconcile ourselves to see the distinctive characteristics of Christ's Hospital effaced, if not soon, at least in the near future".

A contributor to *The Christ's Hospital Book* (1953) described how, on the day the foundation stone was laid in October 1897 by the Prince of Wales, with full masonic ritual, "special trains conveyed the whole school, boys and girls, staff and guests, to West Horsham, where detrainment took place at a siding erected for the occasion. Marquees were provided for the ceremony and for lunch for all, and these temporary structures were the only visible sights in the windswept waste of sticky clay. Few who attended will ever forget how bitterly cold and bleak it was, and many were tempted to wonder whether the consulting engineer might not have been correct in saying that never, in any circumstances, could the Horsham site be a desirable one for a large school".

***

Charles's application for entry to Christ's Hospital, submitted by John Lamb on behalf of his younger son, read simply, "Petitioner has a wife and three children, and he finds it difficult to maintain and educate his family without some assistance". In addition, a guarantor for the sum of £100 against loss or damage incurred to the school by the prospective pupil, also had to be found, as a condition of entry. Not surprisingly, Salt arranged for somebody to put up the money, although he did not directly assume this responsibility himself.

On his arrival at Christ's Hospital, Charles met another new boy; someone who would subsequently become a lifelong friend. Samuel Taylor Coleridge – the future author of *Kubla Khan* and *The Rime of the Ancient Mariner* – was the son of a clergyman with a very large family to support. Their home was at Ottery St. Mary in Devon, but everything changed for Coleridge in October 1781 when he was eight, following his father's death. Originally destined for Charterhouse, he found himself at Christ's Hospital instead and arrived in London following a brief spell at the junior branch of the school in Hertford, "[where] I was very happy on the whole", he recalled, "for I had plenty to eat and drink, and we had pudding and vegetables almost every day. I remained there six weeks, and then was drafted up to the great school in London, where I arrived in September 1782...". He was just over two years older than Charles but, despite the difference in their ages (quite a considerable gap in boys so young), they soon became firm friends. There was a degree of hero-worship in Charles's affection for Coleridge; a boy who affected a lost and dreamy persona at school. Despite his air of lofty detachment, however, he was soon recognised among his peers for his literary precociousness and magnetic oratorical ability. Even as a schoolboy he could hold his audience entranced; a skill that he would employ to great effect in the years ahead. "Come back into memory," wrote Charles in 1820, "like thou wert in the day-spring of thy fancies, with hope like a fiery column before thee, Samuel Taylor Coleridge. How have I seen the casual passer through the cloisters stand still, entranced with admiration to hear thee unfold in thy deep and sweet intonations the mysteries of Plotinus, or reciting Homer in his Greek, or Pindar, while the walls of the old Grey Friars re-echoed to the accents of the inspired charity-boy!"

Coleridge's total self-absorption on such occasions, when he became so consumed by his own eloquence that he was sometimes oblivious to an audience, could become a source of irritation even to his closest friends, as he grew older and increasingly didactic. Even Charles, probably his most faithful and tolerant disciple, could not resist satirising his friend, as he does in this account of a wholly fictitious meeting which supposedly took place in their later years; a fiction, however, which nevertheless contains a grain of truth! Charles was on his way to the City one day (no doubt going to work at the East India House,) when he bumped into Coleridge, "brimful of some new idea, and in spite of my assuring him that time was precious, he drew me within the door of an unoccupied garden. He took me by the button of my coat and, closing his eyes, commenced an eloquent discourse, waving his right hand gently. The striking of a clock recalled me to a sense of duty. I saw it was of no use to attempt to break away so… taking my penknife I quietly severed the button from my coat and decamped. Five hours afterwards, in passing the same garden, on my way home, I heard Coleridge's voice, and on looking in there he was, with closed eyes – the button in his fingers – and his right hand gracefully waving, just as when I left him. He had never missed me!".

***

Leigh Hunt's description of the school routine at Christ's Hospital would have been readily familiar to Charles. "We rose at the call of a bell, at six in summer, and seven in winter," he wrote, "and after combing ourselves, and washing our hands and faces, went, at the call of another bell to breakfast. All this took up about an hour. From breakfast we proceeded to school, where we remained till eleven, winter and summer, and then had an hour's play. Dinner took place at twelve. Afterwards was a little play till one, when we again went to school, and remained till five in summer and four in winter. At six was the supper. We used to play after it in summer till eight. In winter we proceeded from supper to bed."

Coleridge, in a letter to his West Country friend, Thomas Poole, complained that the school diet "was very scanty. Every morning a bit of dry bread and some bad small beer". ("Our quarter of a penny loaf – our 'crug'," – as Charles described it in his Elia essay, *Christ's Hospital Five-and-Thirty Years Ago* (1820), "moistened with attenuated small beer, in wooden piggins, smacking of the pitched leathern jack it was poured from".) "Every evening a larger piece of bread," Coleridge continued, "and cheese or butter, whichever we liked. For dinner: on Sunday, boiled beef and broth; Monday: bread and butter, milk and water," and so it continued in this cheerless and meagre vein throughout the week. "Our appetites were damped, never satisfied, and we had no vegetable." Leigh Hunt confirmed that they were given meat for dinner every other day, "and that consisting of a small slice, such as would be given to an infant three or four years old. Yet even that, with all our hunger, was very often left half-eaten, the meat was so tough".

Charles, however, fared somewhat better. Although he was a boarder at Christ's Hospital, he was allowed to go home occasionally for brief visits during term time, as the Temple was so close at hand. "His schoolfellows indulged him, the masters were fond of him and he was given special privileges not known to others," explained Martin, although why this should have been the case is unclear. It is true that he was regarded as a gentle soul with an engaging manner; he also possessed a slight stammer, but these are not attributes that would necessarily mark him out for special favour. Nevertheless, at school "he had his tea and hot rolls o' mornings", Martin continued, "and his ancient aunt used to toddle there to bring him good things when he, schoolboy-like, only despised her for it".

Much later, in a letter to Coleridge of early February 1797, written as the old lady lay dying, Charles confessed that he "used to be ashamed to see her come and sit herself down on the coal-hole steps… and open her apron, and bring out her basin with some nice thing she had caused to be saved for me". In the Elian version of events, Charles wrote in his essay on Christ's Hospital, "I remember the good old relative squatting down upon some odd stone in a by-nook of the cloisters, disclosing the viands… There was love for the bringer; shame for the thing brought, and the manner of its bringing; sympathy for those who were too many to share in it; and, at top of all, hunger… predominant, breaking down the stony fences of shame, and awkwardness, and a troubling over-consciousness."

On one particular occasion, however, Aunt Hetty's kindness resulted in a sense of deep remorse. "My good old aunt, who never parted from me at the end of a holiday without stuffing a sweetmeat or some nice thing into my pocket, had dismissed me one evening with a smoking plum cake, fresh from the oven,"

Charles related in his Elia essay, *A Dissertation upon Roast Pig* (1822). On the way back to school he gave away the cake to a beggar he encountered on London Bridge. "I walked on a little, buoyed up, as one is on such occasions… but before I got to the end of the bridge, my better feelings returned, and I burst into tears, thinking how ungrateful I had been to my good old aunt, to go and give her good gift away to a stranger… and then I thought of the pleasure my aunt would be taking in thinking that I – I myself, and not another – would eat her nice cake and how disappointed she would feel that I had never had a bit if it in my mouth at last."

***

What kind of boy was Charles when he first entered Christ's Hospital? No doubt he would have been immediately aware – and quite possibly overawed by the fact – that his new school was a decidedly more elevated seat of learning than Mrs. Reynolds's homely schoolroom, or Bird's unprepossessing academy. He was, wrote his schoolfellow, Charles Valentine LeGrice, "an amiable, gentle boy, very sensible and keenly observing, indulged by his schoolfellows and by his master on account of his infirmity of speech. His countenance was mild, his complexion clear brown… His step was plantigrade, which made his walk slow and peculiar, adding to the staid appearance of his figure. I never heard his name mentioned without the addition of Charles, although as there was no other boy by the name of Lamb the addition was unnecessary; but there was an implied kindness in it, and it was a proof that his gentle manners excited that kindness.

"His delicate frame and his difficulty of utterance, which was increased by agitation, unfitted him for joining in any boisterous sport. The description which he gives, in his *Recollections of*

Christ's Hospital, of the habits and feelings of the schoolboy, is a true one in general, but is more particularly a delineation of himself – the feelings were all in his own heart – the portrait was his own: 'While others were all fire and play, he stole along with all the self-concentration of a young monk.'."

The monastic allusion is apt. Charles would have been in a minority – perhaps unique – among his schoolfellows for having his family home in the ancient and cloistered setting of the Temple, while at the same time going to school in the similarly cloistered surroundings of Christ's Hospital. He could walk between these two insulated worlds in less than a quarter of an hour and did so twice a week during term time on the two half-holidays. "In ten minutes he was in the gardens, on the terrace, or at the fountain of the Temple," wrote LeGrice, "here was his home, here his recreation…". Perhaps his immersion in these venerable surroundings helped to foster his reputation among masters and fellow pupils alike as that of an old-fashioned child.

That Charles was proud to have been a 'Blue-Coat Boy' is clear from his essay, *Recollections of Christ's Hospital*, which first appeared in the *Gentleman's Magazine* in 1813 (seven years prior to his Elian account of his old school). "The Christ's Hospital boy feels that he is no charity boy," he declared, "he feels it in the antiquity and regality of the foundation to which he belongs; in the usage which he meets with at school, and the treatment he is accustomed to out of its bounds; in the respect, and even kindness, which his well-known garb never fails to procure him in the streets of the metropolis; he feels it in his education, in that measure of classical attainments which every individual at that school, though not destined to a learned profession, has it in his power to procure – attainments which it would be worse than folly to put in the reach of the labouring classes to acquire; he feels it in the numberless comforts, and even magnificencies, which surround him; in his old and awful cloisters, with their traditions; in his spacious schoolrooms, and in the well-ordered, airy and lofty rooms where he sleeps; in his stately dining-hall, hung round with pictures... one of them surpassing in size and grandeur almost any other in the kingdom; above all in the very extent and magnitude of the body to which he belongs, and the consequent spirit, the intelligence, the public conscience, which is the result of so many various yet wonderfully combining members... The Christ's Hospital or 'Blue-Coat' boy has a distinctive character of his own, as far removed from the abject qualities of a common charity-boy as it is from the disgusting forwardness of a lad brought up at some other of the public schools. His very garb, as it is antique and venerable, feeds his self-respect."

Charles relished, too, both the traditions and ceremonial aspects of his school. "Our transcending superiority in those invigorating sports, leap-frog and basting the bear; our delightful excursions in the summer holidays to the New River near Newington, where, like otters, we would live the long day in the water, never caring for dressing ourselves when we had once stripped; our savoury meals afterwards, when we came home almost famished with staying out all day without our dinners; our visits to the Tower where, by ancient privilege, we had free access to all the curiosities; our solemn processions through the City at Easter, with the Lord Mayor's largesse of buns, wine and a shilling, with the festive questions and civic pleasantries of the dispensing Aldermen, which were more to us than all the rest of the banquet; our stately suppings in public, where the well-lighted hall, and the confluence of well-dressed company who came to see us, made the whole look more like a concert or assembly than a scene of plain bread-and-cheese collation...

"Nor would I willingly forget any of these things that administered to our vanity. The hem-stitched bands and town-made shirts, which some of the most fashionable among us wore; the town-girdles, with buckles of silver or shining stone; the badges of the sea-boys; the cots, or superior shoe-strings of the monitors...".

These early experiences would have been important milestones in developing and cementing Charles's love for his native city. From a young age he would no doubt have heartily endorsed Dr. Johnson's oft-quoted maxim that "When a man is tired of London, he is tired of life; for there is in London all that life can afford".

***

Charles proved himself to be a diligent scholar during his seven years at Christ's Hospital. By the time he left, a few months before his fifteenth birthday, he was able to read Greek, and had an excellent grasp of Latin composition. He was also particularly well-versed in the English classics by this time (in part, no doubt, by courtesy of the freedom he enjoyed in exploring Salt's library). Even at this young age, he was drawn especially to the Elizabethan dramatists; above all Shakespeare, whose plays, he later claimed, were "the strangest and sweetest food of his mind from infancy". Charles's own earliest literary effort, of which we are aware at least, is a set of stanzas written while he was still at school. They were preserved in a manuscript book which was reserved specifically for those pupils' exercises which were considered to be of "more than ordinary merit". Written in 1789, there were six stanzas in all, the first of which ran:

> *What time in bands of slumber all were laid,*
> *To Death's dark court, methought I was convey'd;*
> *In realms it lay far hid from mortal sight,*
> *And gloomy tapers scarce kept out the night.*

Charles progressed in due course to become one of the school's Deputy Grecians, which was confirmation of his proficiency in Greek. It is possible that he would have become a fully fledged Grecian in time, were it not for the slight impediment in his speech. Public speaking formed part of a Grecian's duties on the school's annual Speech Day; an address given before an audience comprising not only the entire school, but also parents and local worthies too. "The Grecians were quite a class apart," recalled one former pupil, "very superior persons indeed. We never dreamed of addressing one of them; if one spoke to us it was considered to be an honour… They had a special gait as they walked, known as 'spadging'; a longish stride with a dip of the whole body in the middle of the pace. The graciousness of their movements was much enhanced by the voluminous swaying of their coats. These were of a cut rather longer in proportion than our own… We all looked upon Grecians as a kind of god. They were never aggressive towards us, the lower fry."

The literary editor and critic, John Middleton Murry, who was a pupil at Christ's Hospital during the first decade of the twentieth century, described how in Charles's and Coleridge's day, the Grecians were "the lords of the school… With his velvet cuffs, his multitudinous buttons, with his coat of superfine cloth, and his gracefully drooping girdle, he sat on the polished granite stones, plumb in the middle of the Grecians' cloister, itself plumb in the centre of the school. He was, indeed, the cynosure of every eye, the observed of all observers: he was more, he was the centre of the life of the school."

The majority of Grecians eventually entered the Church. Thus, even had Charles received the most prestigious accolade that Christ's Hospital could bestow on one of its pupils, his slight stammer might well have discouraged him from pursuing a career that would have inevitably included frequent orations from the pulpit. The poet William Wordsworth, who would later become one of Charles's friends, wrote of him that "he was a good Latin scholar, and probably would have gone to college upon one of the school's foundations, but for the impediment in his speech".

As it was, Charles left school on the 23rd of November 1789, a few months short of his fifteenth birthday, and many long years of toil in the mundane workaday world awaited him. He always looked back upon his time at Christ's Hospital with great fondness. He would return to the school occasionally, to meet and speak to the newest crop of boys. Leigh Hunt wrote, "Lamb's visits to the school I remember well, with his fine intelligent face. Little did I think I should have the pleasure of sitting with it in after-times as an old friend, and seeing it careworn and still finer."

At this early stage in his life, of course, Charles could not possibly have envisaged that, in years to come, two of the school's houses would be named after him when Christ's Hospital moved out of London; nor that a Charles Lamb prize would be awarded annually to the best English essayist among the 'Blue-Coat Boys'. It comprised a Lamb medal, originally struck in 1875 to mark the centenary of his birth and became much-coveted. Murry competed for the medal during his time at the school. "One of these medals was in the school museum, and I had long admired it," he wrote in the *Christ's Hospital Book* (1953). "Indeed, it is a beautiful thing… It was a simple silver medal, unaccompanied by any wad of calf-bound volumes. And that appealed to me. It was as near as one could get to the straightforward Greek wreath of bays which was appropriately part of the design of the medal itself. But most of all I desired it because it was struck in honour of Charles Lamb, whom I had now begun to read and admire, and to consider the noblest and most human of all 'Old Blues'."

Chapter Three

'I Shall See Her Again in Heaven'

Mary Field's gravestone in the old churchyard at Widford

While a proportion of Charles's school friends and contemporaries would have been destined either to receive a university education or to take Holy Orders, when their own turn came to leave Christ's Hospital Charles, on the other hand, merely swapped one desk for another. He did not complain; indeed, he appeared to make the transition seamlessly. His first spell of employment came about through a fortuitous connection at the Temple: an old lawyer named Thomas Coventry. Lucas describes him as a friend or [another] patron of the Lamb family who, like his associate, Salt, was also a Governor of Christ's Hospital. As such, he was well-placed to recommend Charles for employment among his many and varied business connections. He would also have been a familiar sight to the young Charles while he was growing up in the Temple. "[Coventry] passed his youth in contracted circumstances, which gave him early those parsimonious habits which in after life never forsook him," explained Charles, in his Elia essay, *The Old Benchers of the Inner Temple* (1820), "so that with one windfall or another, about the time I knew him he was master of four or five hundred thousand pounds; nor did he look, or walk, worth a moidore less. He lived in a gloomy house opposite the pump in Serjeants' Inn, Fleet Street... [His] person was a quadrate, his step massy and elephantine, his face square as the lion's, his gait peremptory and path-keeping, indivertible from his way as a moving column, the scarecrow of his inferiors, the brow-beater of equals and superiors, who made a solitude of children wherever he came, for they fled his insufferable presence, as they would have shunned an Elisha bear. His growl was as thunder in their ears, whether he spake to them in mirth or in rebuke, his invitatory notes being, indeed, of all, the most repulsive and horrid."

Coventry's commanding and off-putting demeanour was made fiercer by his lavish and excessive use of snuff. "Clouds of snuff, aggravating the natural terrors of his speech broke from each majestic nostril, darkening the air. He took it, not by pinches, but a palmful at once, diving for it under the mighty flaps of his old-fashioned waistcoat pocket; his waistcoat red and angry, his coat dark rapee, tinctured by dye original, and by adjuncts with buttons of obsolete gold. And so he paced the terrace [of the Temple.]" (It is worth noting here, perhaps, that both Charles and Mary were prodigious takers of a 'stimulating pinch' throughout their adult lives.) "[Coventry] had an agreeable seat at North Cray," Charles continued, "where he seldom spent above a day or two at a time in the summer; but preferred, during the hot months, standing at his window, in this damp, close, well-like mansion, to watch, as he said, 'the maids drawing water all day long.' I suspect he had his within-door reasons for the preference... He might think his treasures more safe. His house had the aspect of a strong box... His housekeeping was severely looked after, but he kept the table of a gentleman. He would know who came in and who went out of his house, but his kitchen chimney was never suffered to freeze."

It would seem that not long before Charles was due to leave Christ's Hospital, Coventry approached one of his friends, a City merchant named Joseph Paice, in the hope of obtaining employment for his young protege. A menial post in Paice's counting house had recently fallen vacant; Charles was offered the job and accepted it without hesitation. Paice made a lasting and favourable impression on his young employee. More than thirty years later, in his Elia essay, *Modern Gallantry* (1822), he recalled Paice with an obvious and deep respect. "Joseph Paice, of Bread Street Hill, merchant, and one of the Directors of the South-Sea Company," he wrote, "was the only pattern of consistent gallantry I have met with. He took me under his shelter at an early age, and bestowed some pains upon me. I owe to his precepts and example whatever there is of the man of business (and that is not much) in my composition. It is not his fault that I did not prosper more. Though bred a Presbyterian, and brought up a merchant, he was the finest gentleman of his time. He had not one system of attention to females in the drawing-room and another in the shop or at the stall. I do not mean that he made no distinction. But he never lost sight of sex, or overlooked it in the casualties of a disadvantageous situation. I have seen him stand bare-headed to a poor servant girl, while she had been enquiring of him the way to some street, in such a posture of unforced civility as neither to embarrass her in the acceptance, nor himself in the offer of it... I have seen him tenderly escorting a market-woman, whom he had encountered in a shower, exalting his umbrella over her poor basket of fruit, that it might receive no damage, with as much carefulness as if she had been a countess."

Charles was fortunate indeed to fall so early in his life into such benevolent hands. At Paice's funeral in September 1810, the officiating pastor declared, "[Paice's] attention to the feelings of others, in the common intercourse of life, so far exceeded the common standard, and must sometimes have proved so inconvenient to himself, that those who were unacquainted with his real character, or destitute of any resemblance to it, were almost ready to doubt his sincerity; while those who knew him best, from their intimate acquaintance with his habitual temper, gave him full credit for even kinder feelings than he expressed."

It is impossible to say, with any degree of certainty, how long Charles remained at Paice's counting house. However, we do know that on the 1st of September 1791 he began work as a clerk at the South-Sea House, then situated at one end of Threadneedle Street in the City. By this time he was sixteen and a half. It is probable that, through his influence as one of the company's directors, Paice took a hand in securing this position for Charles whose older brother, John, was already well-established in the firm. (John spent his entire working life at the South-Sea House, in fact, and enjoyed a highly successful career there in the process.)

The building which housed the company's headquarters was deeply impressive from an architectural point of view, as befitted the colonial aspirations that had given rise to it. "Stately porticoes, imposing staircases, offices roomy as the state apartments in palaces," was how Charles described its opulence in his inaugural Elia essay, *The South-Sea House* (1820). "The oaken wainscots hung with pictures of deceased governors and sub-governors, of Queen Anne… huge charts, which subsequent discoveries have antiquated; dusty maps of Mexico, dim as dreams… The long passages hung with buckets, appended, in idle row, to walls, whose substance might defy any, short of the last conflagration – with vast ranges of cellarage under all, where dollars and pieces of eight once lay – long since dissipated, or scattered into air at the blast of that famous BUBBLE. Such is the South-Sea House." (The fortunes of the South-Sea Company had risen ever higher, and many were those who invested heavily in – or gambled on – the continued increasing success of its shares. By the autumn of 1720, however, the value of the company's stock plummeted, when it was discovered that there were not sufficient funds to pay out investors, and public confidence in the company swiftly evaporated. Stockholders lost their investments and many people were ruined, having lost their entire fortunes in the process. The so-called 'bubble' had well and truly burst. Stability and confidence in the company were eventually restored by Robert Walpole, who became Prime Minister the following year.)

The 'South-Sea Bubble', as this infamous event became known, was sixty years in the past when Charles joined the company as a humble junior clerk but, as he intimated in his recollections of the South-Sea House, his erstwhile colleagues seemed to operate in another kind of bubble of their own making! "The very clerks which I remember… had an air very different from those in the public offices that I have had to do with since. They partook of the genius of the place," he wrote. "They were mostly bachelors. Generally (for they had not much to do), persons of a curious and speculative turn of mind… they were of all descriptions; and, not having been brought together in early life (which has a tendency to assimilate the members of corporate bodies to each other), but, for the most part, placed in this house in ripe or middle age they necessarily carried into it their separate habits and oddities, unqualified, if I may so speak, as into a common stock. Hence they formed a sort of Noah's Ark. Odd fishes. A lay-monastery. Domestic retainers in a great house, kept more for show than use. Yet pleasant fellows, full of chat – and not a few among them had arrived at considerable proficiency on the German flute."

Having conjured up many a vivid and quirky portrait of his former comrades, composed thirty or so years after the event, Lucas described it as "one of the most remarkable feats in literature of what might be called imaginative memory". After all, who would not like to have met Evans, the cashier: "…a Cambro-Britain [who] had something of the choleric complexion of his countrymen stamped on his visage, but was a worthy sensible man at bottom. He wore his hair, to the last, powdered and fizzed out, in the fashion which I remember to have seen in caricatures of what were termed, in my young days, 'Maccaronies'. He was the last of that race of beaux. Melancholy as a gib-cat over his counter all the forenoon, I think I see him making up his cash (as they call it) with tremulous fingers, as if he feared everyone about him was a defaulter; in his hypochondry ready to imagine himself one; haunted, at least, with the idea of the possibility of his becoming one; his tristful visage clearing up a little over his roast neck of veal at Anderton's at two (where his picture still hangs, taken a little before his death by desire of the master of the coffee-house, which he had frequented for the last five-and-twenty-years), but not attaining the meridian of its animation till evening brought on the hour of tea and visiting. The simultaneous sound of his well-known rap at the door with the stroke of the clock announcing six, was a topic of never-failing mirth in the families which this dear old bachelor gladdened with his presence. Then was his forte, his glorified hour! How he would chirp and expand over a muffin! How would he dilate into secret history! His countryman Pennant himself, in particular, could not be more eloquent than he in relation to old and new London – the site of old theatres, churches, streets gone to decay, where Rosamond's pond stood, the Mulberry Gardens, and the Conduit in Cheap – with many a pleasant anecdote… of those grotesque figures which Hogarth has immortalised in his picture of 'Noon'."

What a life, what a personality in all its fine detail, is encompassed in Charles's incomparable vignette of Evans.

Charles was put to work in the Examiner's Office at a salary of half a guinea (55p) per week. In the event, he remained at the South-Sea House for a mere five months, but the world of literature is incomparably the richer as a result of his brief tenure there.

Having left his job with the South-Sea Company at the beginning of February 1792 (two days before his seventeenth birthday), Charles started work on the 5th of April with the East India Company, at their headquarters – East India House – in Leadenhall Street, close to his previous office. It is not entirely clear why Charles left the South-Sea Company after such a short time. It is possible the post was a temporary one, or that he sought better terms and conditions of employment elsewhere. Given the time that was to elapse between one job and the next, however, he obviously did not have a new post to take up straight away. Lucas speculates that Charles may well have taken advantage of this interval of unemployment to visit his grandmother at Blakesware. If so, it was probably the last time he stayed at the house, given that Mary Field died during the summer. It is also likely that this Hertfordshire interlude witnessed the birth or acceleration of Charles's passion for Ann Simmons of nearby Blenheims.

The Lamb family's reliable old benefactor, Salt, who died in July 1792, may have intended to play some part in securing this new appointment for his friend and servant's younger son in the East India Company's accounts department. However, Paice stepped in to become Charles's benefactor on this occasion. He had some influence with the East India Board, through his personal friendship with the company's chairman. As a probationary clerk, Charles received no pay at all for the first three years of his employment (one can only wonder how he managed to survive financially in the meantime!) but, from April 1795, his salary was set at £40 per annum rising to £70 the following year. The company also provided regular opportunities for their employees' advancement. Charles was to remain (not always contentedly) at the East India House until his retirement, thirty-three years after taking up his appointment.

***

Following Salt's death, it became necessary, in his absence, for the Lambs to move from the Temple; the only family home that Charles had ever known. It was a place that he loved and where he felt secure. Salt's kindness and benevolence towards the Lambs continued to be felt by them, however, even after his death. He left £500 in South-Sea stock to John Lamb, "who has lived with me near forty years", plus a couple of annuities which yielded a tiny annual sum; while to Elizabeth he left two separate amounts of £100 each; one of which, he explained in his will, "was well deserved for her care and attention during my illness". These were generous bequests indeed for people in the Lambs' condition of life but, the fact that they were now obliged to leave the Temple still fell like a hammer-blow upon them.

The exact whereabouts of the Lambs' new home are uncertain but, by 1794, they were occupying lodgings necessarily somewhat inferior to those to which for so long they had been accustomed. No. 7 Little Queen Street was an unprepossessing thoroughfare at the close of the eighteenth century. It ran south from High Holborn in the area of the present-day Kingsway, and no longer exists. The teeming and noisome street (located on the edge of a notorious red light district), would have certainly provided a jarring and unwelcome contrast to the sedate and cloistered atmosphere of the Temple, barely half a mile away. For Charles, Crown Office Row might just as well have been on the other side of the world. John Lamb junior was not living with his family by this time, but Mary – now employed at home as a mantua-maker – certainly shared in the cramped quarters.

However, Charles would probably not have spent very much time in his new confined surroundings. During the week, he was in his office all day at the East India House, and his evenings were usually passed, like those of many a young man of his age, enjoying himself in public houses and taverns. At the end of 1794, for example, he could be found on most evenings consuming egg-hot (a hot drink made from beer, eggs, sugar and nutmeg), and smoking Oronooko, in the company of his old Christ's Hospital schoolfriend, Coleridge, at the Salutation and Cat, a coaching inn situated in Newgate Street, and subsequently destroyed by fire in 1833. By a happy coincidence, the building stood nearly opposite to their old school. Coleridge had gone up to Jesus College, Cambridge, after leaving Christ's Hospital, but he was currently residing temporarily in London lodgings, having abandoned his university degree.

During the summer and autumn of 1794, in fact, Coleridge had spent much of his time with another young poet, Robert Southey, who was then studying at Oxford. They were concocting a plan between them of establishing a democratic commune on the banks of the Susquehanna River in Pennysylvania. The scheme, which grew quickly in its scope and momentum, was called Pantisocracy; a venture, it was envisaged, that would comprise twelve young gentlemen and twelve young ladies, all living in perfect harmony on the land, and with each member of the group having an equal share in the government of the enterprise. It was an intensely idealistic vision, originally born of two passionate young men in the heat of full-throated summer. However, as the autumn and winter wore on, any real prospect of Pantisocracy coming to fruition declined with the seasons, and the dream evaporated before anyone involved had even embarked for the Susquehanna.

Dr. Johnson famously said, "As soon as I enter the door of a tavern, I experience oblivion of care, and a freedom from solicitude. There is nothing which has yet been contrived by man, by which so much happiness is produced as by a good tavern or inn." No doubt the Salutation and Cat served this function for Charles and Coleridge. The two friends met frequently, talking animatedly until – and probably long after – closing time. Much of their conversation would have been about politics and poetry. These were the years, after all, of the French Revolutionary Wars, but poetry – a shared passion – probably won the day on most occasions. No doubt it was Coleridge's voice that was mainly heard. Always delighting in the past, Charles would have been naturally drawn to the Salutation and Cat; a tavern steeped in history where, reputedly, Sir Christopher Wren would come in to sit with his pipe and a pot of ale during the rebuilding of his masterpiece, St. Paul's Cathedral nearby, following the Great Fire of London in 1666. The task was eventually completed in 1710.

The eighteenth-century novelist, Samuel Richardson, author of *Pamela* (1740/41) and *Clarissa* (1747/48), was said to have been another Christ's Hospital boy, although his attendance at the school cannot be substantiated. However, long before Charles's and Coleridge's day, he had been a regular attender at the Salutation and Cat during the 1730s.

Coleridge introduced Charles to twenty-year-old Southey one evening at the Salutation and Cat and, thereafter, the three of them would often convene in a small back room. "I imagine to myself that little smoky room…" Lamb wrote later, "where we have sat together through the winter nights, beguiling the cares of life with poesy… that nice little smoky room which is even now continually presenting itself to my recollection, with all its associated train of pipes, tobacco, egg-hot, Welsh-rabbit [sic], metaphysics and poetry."

Martin wrote that "the wary landlord, to whom Coleridge's rhapsodies were quite unintelligible, yet who fully understood their value in drawing a knot of thirsty listeners, offered the Talker free quarters for life, if he would stay and talk!". (A similar gesture was made by the redoubtable Muriel Belcher, presiding genius of the Colony Room Club in Soho, when she became its proprietor after the Second World War. She offered the charismatic – and frequently drunk – artist Francis Bacon permanent free drinks every time he made his way up the dingy narrow staircase and through the green baize door that was the club's entrance, because he always attracted so many paying customers in his wake!)

Another favoured haunt of Charles, Coleridge and Southey was the Feathers, which Martin described as "a dirty, dingy, delightful tavern, as I have seen it, in Hand Court, Holborn, nearly opposite the Great Turnstile leading into Lincoln's Inn Fields". Situated thus, it was only a few steps away from Charles's front door.

***

In January 1795, Coleridge and Southey left London and made for Bristol, where the two friends wrote poetry and prepared lectures at the same table in their cramped College Street lodgings. Meanwhile, at home in London, Charles felt solitary and deflated. "I felt a dismal void in my heart," he wrote eighteen months later in a letter to Coleridge (by which time Southey and Coleridge had quarrelled bitterly and Pantisocracy was a thing of the past). "[I] found myself cut off at one and the same time from the two most dear to me." Of course, Charles and Coleridge inhabited two very different worlds. In a literary sense, Charles regarded himself as an amateur and Coleridge as a professional man of letters. Charles earned his income by working in an office, and the only writing he was able to do had to be squeezed into an hour or two before he went to work in the morning or when he returned home in the evening, either from work or from the tavern. Beyond that, he could devote more hours to his poetry and reading during his rare periods of annual leave. He possessed an equable temperament and a quiet demeanour; his life was ordered and filled with routine. Coleridge, on the other hand, had a mercurial personality, coupled with an emotional and romantic life of unbridled chaos; all of it fuelled by copious draughts of laudanum and opium. Domesticity, conventional or otherwise, did not sit easily with him.

Charles described Coleridge as "an archangel, a little damaged". "It was a characteristically charitable judgement. Coleridge was, in fact, very damaged indeed," according to Alan Hankinson in *Coleridge Walks the Fells* (1993 ed.). "In temperament: irresolute and irresponsible; incapable, for the most part, of adult self-discipline; dominating and demanding; full of high-sounding sentiments which his actions immediately belied; constantly outlining grandiose work plans that were doomed to come to nothing. He could not keep appointments. If he did keep them he might be hours late. For all his widely recognised qualities as poet and preacher, lecturer and journalist, he could not make enough money to meet the basic needs of his family. Although everyone found Coleridge amazing and fascinating at first, those who lived in close daily contact with him soon found that he was always difficult, sometimes impossible."

***

When Charles wrote to Coleridge, complaining that he felt the absence of the two people most dear to him, it was not Southey to whom he was also referring (Charles barely knew him at that stage), but Ann Simmons, tucked away at distant Blenheims in Hertfordshire. This, after all, had been the period of his ultimately hopeless love for her; a chapter in his life which ended with their permanent separation (although how much time they ever spent actually in each other's company is a moot point).

"You came to Town, and I saw you at a time when your heart was yet bleeding with recent wounds. Like yourself, I was sore galled with disappointed Hope." Perhaps these words, written to Coleridge during the summer of 1796, suggest that Charles still loved Ann or, as Lucas concluded, "loved to dwell tenderly… upon all that she stood for in his mind… remembering that he was only twenty-one, that he was solitary, that he was proposing to be a poet, and that his hero, Coleridge, had long cherished a grand passion; but I do not fancy that his original boyish fervour ever revived". A sonnet, which Charles claimed to have written during a visit to Hertfordshire in the early summer of 1795, gives a flavour of his yearning retrospective love:

When last I roved these winding wood walks green,
Green winding walks and pathways shady-sweet,
Oftentimes would Anna seek the silent scene,
Shrouding her beauties in the lone retreat.
No more I hear her footsteps in the shade;

Her image only in these pleasant ways
Meets me self-wandering where in better days
I held free converse with my fair-haired maid.

That his doomed love for Ann had been at least partly to blame for driving Charles beyond the limits of his sanity, we can infer from a letter that he wrote to Coleridge in May 1796: "The six weeks that finished last year and began this, your very humble servant spent very agreeably in a madhouse at Hoxton. I am got somewhat rational now, and don't bite anyone. But mad I was; and many a vagary my imagination played with me, enough to make a volume, if all were told. My sonnets I have extended to the number of nine since I saw you, and will some day communicate to you. I am beginning a poem in blank verse which, if I finish, I publish… Coleridge, it may convince you of my regards for you when I tell you my head ran on you, in my madness, as much almost as on another person, who I am inclined to think was the more immediate cause of my temporary frenzy."

Charles's thoughts ran on his sister, Mary, too and he addressed a sonnet to her, "written in my prison-house in one of my lucid intervals":

…Thou to me didst ever show
Kindest affection; and wouldst oft-times lend
An ear to the desponding love-sick boy,
Weeping my sorrows with me, who repay
But ill the mighty debt of love I owe,
Mary, to thee, my sister and my friend.

If, as seems likely, Ann Simmons was indeed the principal cause of Charles's stay in the asylum at Hoxton, it would be perhaps instructive to examine the background to his life in general around this time. He worked all day at his desk in the East India

House, entering endless columns of figures in huge ledgers; an occupation of leaden tedium for a young man whose natural bent lay overwhelmingly in the direction of literature and the theatre. He told Coleridge that he was "the only friend I have in the world. I go nowhere, and have no acquaintance. Slow of speech, and reserved of manners, no one seeks or cares for my society; and I am left alone".

Responding to this catalogue of woes, Coleridge invited Charles and Mary to visit him but Charles's reply, dated the 1st of July, tells its own story. "The first moment I can come I will; but my hopes of coming yet a while hang on a ticklish thread. The coach I come by is immaterial, as I shall so easily, by your direction, find ye out. My mother is grown so entirely helpless (not having any use of her limbs) that Mary is necessarily confined from ever sleeping out, she being her bed-fellow. She thanks you though, and will accompany me in spirit… I possibly may not come this fortnight; therefore all thou hast to do is not to look for me any particular day, only to write word immediately, if at any time you quit Bristol… Young Savory, of my office, is suddenly taken ill in this very nick of time, and I must officiate for him till he can come to work again." In fact, it would be a year before Charles could pay a visit to Coleridge.

Martin paints a drab picture of life at the Lambs' cramped lodgings in Little Queen Street at this time. "The family was straightened direfully in means [they were clearly missing Salt's support, despite the largesse they received from him upon his death] and in miserable case in many ways; the mother ailing helplessly, the father decaying rapidly in mind and body; the aged aunt, more of a burden than a help, despite the scanty board she paid; and the sister suffering almost ceaselessly from attacks of her congenital gloom, submitting to the constant toil of her household duties, of her dressmaking, and of nursing her parents."

***

If 1796 could be said to have started badly for Charles, perhaps he would have buckled completely during his spell in the asylum at Hoxton, had he known what lay in store for him and his family before the year was out. A newspaper report which appeared in the *Morning Chronicle* on Monday the 26th of September, relates the tragic events in graphic detail. "On Friday afternoon, the Coroner and a respectable Jury sat on the body of a lady in the neighbourhood of Holborn, who died in consequence of a wound from her daughter the previous day [i.e. Thursday the 22nd of September]. It appeared, by the evidence adduced that, while the family were preparing for dinner, the young lady seized a case-knife lying on the table, and in a menacing manner pursued a little girl, her apprentice, around the room. On the calls of her infirm mother to forbear, she renounced her first object, and with loud shrieks approached her parent. The child, by her cries, quickly brought the landlord to the house, but too late. The dreadful scene presented to him the mother lifeless, pierced to the heart, on a chair, her daughter yet wildly standing over her with the fatal knife, and the old man, her father, weeping by her side, himself bleeding at the forehead, from the effects of a severe blow he had received from one of the forks she had been madly hurling about the room.

"For a few days prior to this, the family had observed some symptoms of insanity in her, which had so much increased on the previous Wednesday evening, that her brother early the next morning went in quest of Dr. Pitcairn – had that gentleman been met with, the fatal catastrophe had, in all probability, been prevented… The Jury, of course, brought in their Verdict, LUNACY."

The situation was rendered all the more tragic, if that were possible, by the fact that Mary had always shown great affection towards her mother. The jury further concluded that the extra burden placed upon Mary by the need for her to attend her mother day and night in her infirmity, and to care for her ailing father also, coupled with the demands of her work as a mantua-maker, led to a temporary loss of her reason. By his own account of events, it would appear that Charles arrived home just at the time the tragedy was unfolding. One newspaper reported that he "came at the child's cries… just in time to disarm his sister, and thus prevent further harm". From that moment, it seems that Charles took command of the situation. "He had to; there was no one else," explained David Cecil, in *A Portrait of Charles Lamb* (1983). "His father was in his dotage; old Aunt Hetty had collapsed, overcome by the horrors which she had witnessed; his brother, John, while professing sympathy, shrank back, determined to be as little involved as possible in so painful an affair. Charles it was, therefore, who had to take responsibility for the Lamb family and its future."

A few days later, on the 27th of September, Charles wrote to Coleridge giving him a brief account of the catastrophe which had so recently overtaken them all at Little Queen Street. "My poor, dear, dearest sister, in a fit of insanity, has been the death of her own mother. I was at hand only time enough to snatch the knife out of her grasp. She is at present in a madhouse, from whence I fear she must be moved to an hospital. God has preserved to me my senses; I eat and drink; and sleep, and have my judgement, I believe, very sound. My poor father was slightly wounded, and I am left to take care of him and my aunt. Mr. Norris, of the Bluecoat [sic] School has been very kind to us, and we have no other friend; but, thank God, I am very calm and composed, and able to do the best that remains to do. Write as religious letter as possible, but no mention of what is gone and done with. With me the former things are passed away… Mention nothing of poetry. I have destroyed every vestige of past vanities of that kind. Do as you please, but if you publish, publish mine (I give free leave) without name or initial, and never send me a book, I charge you. [It had been proposed that Charles should contribute some of his sonnets to a collection of poems by Coleridge, that was due to be published shortly.] Don't think of coming to see me. I will not see you if you come."

A few weeks later, Charles wrote again to Coleridge, this time elaborating on the dreadful scene at home on the evening of the murder. "My aunt was lying insensible – to all appearance like one dying; my father with his poor forehead plaistered [sic] over from a wound he had received from a daughter, dearly loved by him, and who loved him no less dearly; my mother a dead and murdered corpse, in the next room, yet I was wonderfully supported. I closed not my eyes in sleep that night, but lay without terrors and without despair. I have lost no sleep since."

Mary remained in the asylum at Islington, to which she had been originally taken. "The good lady of the madhouse, and her daughter, an elegant, sweet-behaved young lady, love her, and are taken with her amazingly," Charles reported to Coleridge on the 3rd of October, "and I know from [Mary's] own mouth she loves them and longs to be with them as much. Poor thing, they say she was but the other morning saying she knew she must go to Bethlehem for life; that one of her brothers [John] would have it so, but the other would wish it not… that she had often as she passed Bethlem thought it likely, 'here it may be my fate to end my days', conscious of a certain flightiness in her poor head oftentimes, and mindful of more than one severe illness of that nature before."

By the middle of October, Mary seemed composed – even serene – and entirely resigned to her situation, as indicated in a letter that she wrote to Charles at this time. "I have no bad terrifying dreams. At midnight, when I happen to awake, the nurse sleeping by the side of me, I have no fear. The spirit of my mother seems to descend and smile upon me, and bid me to live to enjoy the life and reason which the Almighty has given me. I shall see her again in heaven. She will then understand me better. My grandmother, too, will understand me better, and will then say no more, as she used to do, 'Polly, what are those poor crazy moythered brains of yours thinking of always?'"

Chapter Four

'My Heart Is Quite Sunk'

Coleridge was much troubled when he read of Charles's intention to abandon the writing of poetry; a decision hastily arrived at in the days following his mother's murder. Coleridge's immediate response was to send Charles some lines of his own, newly minted and addressed 'To a Friend Who has Declared His Intention of Writing no more Poetry':

> *Dear Charles! Whilst yet thou wert a babe I ween*
> *That Genius plunged thee in that wizard fount*
> *High Castalie; and (sureties of thy faith)*
> *That Pity and Simplicity stood by.*
> *And promised for thee that thou shouldst renounce*
> *The world's low cares and lying vanities,*
> *Steadfast and rooted in the heavenly Muse,*
> *And washed and sanctified to Poesy...*

Charles told Coleridge at a later date that, in the aftermath of his mother's murder, he had burned all of his own verses. He could be forgiven, perhaps, for having destroyed this unlooked-for effusion from his friend, too, when it arrived; of which there was a great deal more to read before it wound to its tortuous conclusion. Sadly, from the viewpoint of the various biographies that have been written about him over the years, Charles also disposed of a journal that he had kept relating to his innermost thoughts and feelings about Ann Simmons.

However, having nurtured for so long the dream of one day becoming a recognised poet, Charles's literary spirit was somehow rekindled after about a month or six weeks, as a measure of emotional equilibrium slowly settled upon him. Nevertheless, he still endeavoured to keep poesy at arm's length for the time being. "The Fragments I now send you, I want printed to get rid of 'em," he wrote to Coleridge on the 8th of November, "for, while they stick burr-like to my memory they tempt me to go on with the idle trade of versifying, which I long (most sincerely I speak it) I long to leave off, for it is unprofitable to my soul; I feel it is; and these questions about words, and debates about alterations, take me off, I am conscious, from the proper business of my life. Take my sonnets, once for all; and do not propose any reamendments, or mention them again in any shape to me I charge you. I blush that my mind can consider them as things of any worth. And, pray, admit or reject these fragments as you like or dislike them, without ceremony. Call 'em Sketches, Fragments, or what you will; but do not entitle any of my things Love Sonnets, as I told you to call 'em; 'twill only make me look little in my own eyes; for it is a passion of which I retain nothing. 'Twas a weakness… Thank God, the folly has left me for ever."

Four of Charles's sonnets duly appeared in a volume entitled *Poems on Various Subjects* by S.T Coleridge, which was published at the end of 1796. One of Charles's contributions was a sonnet addressed to the celebrated actress of the day, Mrs. Siddons. When it was originally published in the *Morning Chronicle*, it had marked Charles's first appearance in print. This takes us back to those convivial evenings at the Salutation and Cat when Coleridge, according to Lucas, "was writing sonnets to eminent characters for the *Morning Chronicle*", with Charles's help in one of them at least – that addressed to Mrs. Siddons:

> *As when a child on some long Winter's night*
> *Affrighted, clinging to its grandame's knees,*
> *With eager wondering and perturbed delight*
> *Listens strange tales of fearful dark decrees*
> *Muttered to wretch by necromantic spell;*
> *Or of those hags, who, at the witching time*
> *Of murky midnight, ride the air sublime,*
> *And mingle foul embrace with fiends of hell,*
> *Cold horror drinks its blood! Anon the tear*
> *More gentle starts, to hear the beldam tell*
> *Of pretty babes that loved each other dear,*
> *Murdered by cruel uncle's mandate fell:*
> *Ev'n such the shiv'ring joys thy tones impart,*
> *Ev'n so thou, Siddons, meltest my sad heart.*

The authorship of Charles's four sonnets in Coleridge's volume was attributed to 'Charles Lamb of the India House' and the dedication with which he introduced them had an added poignancy given recent events: "The few following poems, creatures of the fancy and the feelings in life's more vacant hours, produced, for the most part, by love in idleness, are, with all a brother's fondness, inscribed to Mary Ann Lamb, the author's best friend and sister."

"This is the pomp and paraphernalia of parting," he told Coleridge in an alliterative flourish, on the 14th of November, "with which I take my leave of a passion which has reigned so royally (so long) within me; thus with its trappings of laureateship, I fling it off, pleased and satisfied with myself that the weakness troubles me no longer. I am wedded, Coleridge, to the fortunes of my sister and my poor old father. Oh my friend! I think sometimes, could I recall the days that are past, which among them should I choose? Not those 'merrier days', not the 'pleasant days of hope', not 'those wanderings with a fair-hair'd maid', which I have so often and so feelingly regretted, but the days, Coleridge, of a mother's fondness for her schoolboy. What would I give to call her back to earth for ONE day! – on my knees to ask her pardon for all those little asperities of temper which, from time to time, have given her gentle spirit pain! – and the day, my friend, I trust, will come. There will be time enough for kind offices of love [and] hereafter her meek spirit shall not reproach me. Oh my friend, cultivate the filial feelings! And let no man think himself released from the kind 'charities' of relationship: these shall give him peace at the last; these are the best foundation for every species of benevolence...".

Charles assumed a coping and capable demeanour in the weeks and months following the tragedy but these words, written to Coleridge, his most intimate friend, reveal the depth of his own pain, but which he kept largely hidden from the world.

Aunt Hetty left the Lambs' lodgings in Little Queen Street soon after the tragedy had occurred and went off to live with a wealthy cousin who offered her a new home, ostensibly on a permanent basis. As a result, when he was not poring over his ledgers at the East India House, Charles was his father's only companion when at home during the evenings. Writing to Coleridge at the beginning of December, he shines a light on the melancholy state of his domestic circumstances during these dark winter months.

"I am starving at the India House, – near seven o'clock without my dinner; and so it has been, and will be, almost all the week. I get home at night o'erwearied, quite faint, and then to cards with my father, who will not let me enjoy a meal in peace; but I must conform to my situation; and I hope I am, for the most part, not unthankful.

"I am got home at last, and, after repeated games at cribbage, have got my father's leave to write awhile; with difficulty got it, for when I expostulated about playing any more, he very aptly replied, 'If you won't play with me, you might as well not come home at all.' The argument was unanswerable, and I set to afresh."

A few days later, in a further letter to Coleridge during the closing month of the year, Charles confessed to his friend that "I almost burned all your letters, – I did as bad, I lent 'em to a friend to keep out of my brother's sight, should he come and make inquisition into our papers; for, much as he dwelt upon your conversation while you were among us, and delighted to be with you, it has been his fashion ever since to depreciate and cry you down; you were the cause of my madness – you and your 'damned foolish sensibility and melancholy'; and he lamented, with a true brotherly feeling, that we ever met... These letters I lent to a friend to be out of the way for a season; but I have claimed 'em in vain, and shall not cease to regret their loss. [No doubt it is a sentiment echoed by many a subsequent literary biographer.] Your packets, posterior to the date of my misfortunes, commencing with that valuable consolatory epistle, are every day accumulating: they are sacred things to me."

Charles also informed Coleridge that Aunt Hetty was about to become a part of the Lamb household once again, in the days leading up to Christmas. "I am beset with perplexities. The old hag of a wealthy relation, who took my aunt off our hands in the beginning of trouble, has found out that she is 'indolent and mulish' – I quote her own words – and that her attachment to us is so strong that she can never be happy apart. The Lady, with delicate irony, remarks that, if I am not an hypocrite, I shall rejoice to receive her again; and that it will be a means of making me more fond of home to have so dear a friend to come home. The fact is, she is jealous of my aunt's bestowing any kind recollections on us while she enjoys the patronage of her roof. She says she finds it inconsistent with her own 'ease and tranquillity', to keep her any longer; and, in fine, summons me to fetch her home. Now, much as I should rejoice to transplant the poor old creature from the chilling air of such patronage, yet I know how straitened we are already, how unable to answer any demand which sickness or any extraordinary expense may make." Aunt Hetty returned to live with Charles and his father, but she would not prove to be an extra mouth to feed for long.

On New Year's Eve 1796, a year that the family must have been pleased to see come to an end, the Lambs moved from 7 Little Queen Street to 45 Chapel Street, Pentonville, a small wooden house on the corner of Liverpool Road, and quite close to the asylum at Islington where Mary was being detained. In the 1790s, Pentonville lay on the northern outskirts of London and, as such, represented for Charles a move away from the centre of town on a scale that he had not previously experienced. Barely two decades earlier, the area was still open countryside until the politician, Henry Penton, embarked upon building an estate of houses on the land and, by that means, became the eponymous founder of Pentonville. It was regarded in Charles's day as a faintly genteel neighbourhood, comprising dwellings for middling clerks and their families and for men in a small way of business. It was, at least, an improvement on their previous lodgings at Little Queen Street. Readers of Charles Dickens will recall that Mr. Brownlow, the saviour of young Oliver Twist, resided in "a quiet shady street near Pentonville", and that comical Mr. Guppy, the lawyer's clerk in *Bleak House* also had lodgings there, "…lowly but airy, open at the back, and considered one of the 'ealthiest outlets".

Unfortunately, further sadness dogged Charles's footsteps and pursued him to his new home, as he related to Coleridge in a letter at the beginning of January 1797: "My poor old aunt, whom you have seen, the kindest, goodest creature to me when I was at school… is now lying on her death-bed. I cannot bear to think on her deplorable state. To the shock she received on that our evil day, from which she never completely recovered, I impute her illness. She says, poor thing, that she is glad she is come home to die with me. I was always her favourite."

In a further letter to Coleridge, dated the 13th of February, Charles was able to conclude his aunt's history. "This afternoon I attend the funeral of my poor old aunt, who died on Thursday. I own I am thankful that the good creature has ended all her days of suffering and infirmity. She was to me the 'cherisher of infancy'… Good God, who could have foreseen all this but four months back! I had reckoned, in particular, on my aunt's living many years; she was a very hearty old woman. But she was a mere skeleton before she died, looked more like a corpse that had lain weeks in the grave, than one fresh dead."

Charles wrote a poem on that day in her memory:

Thou too art dead, very kind
Hast thou been to me in my childish days,
Thou best good creature. I have not forgot
How thou didst love thy Charles, when he was yet
A prating schoolboy; I have not forgot
The busy joy on that important day,
When childlike, the poor wanderer was content
To leave the bosom of parental love,
His childhood's play-place, and his early home,
For the rude fosterings of a stranger's hand,
Hard uncouth tasks, and schoolboy's scanty fare.
How did thine eye peruse him round and round,

> *And hardly knew him in his yellow coats,*
> *Red leathern belt, and gown of russet blue!*
> *Farewell, good aunt!*
> *Go thou, and occupy the same grave-bed*
> *Where the dead mother lies.*

The poem was subsequently included in *Blank Verse*, a collaborative volume with poet and friend, Charles Lloyd, which was published in 1798. The volume is of particular interest, because it also contained the first appearance in print of his most enduring and much-anthologised poem, *The Old Familiar Faces*:

> *I have had playmates, I have had companions,*
> *In my days of childhood, in my joyful school-days –*
> *All, all are gone, the old familiar faces…*
> *I loved a love once, fairest among women.*
> *Closed are her doors on me, I must not see her –*
> *All, all are gone, the old familiar faces…*

***

A welcome respite from his troubles presented itself to Charles in the summer of 1797. During the previous winter, Coleridge had settled (if that were a word one could ever really apply to him) with his wife, Sara, and their young son Hartley, into a small, thatched cottage at Nether Stowey, a Somerset village set in the Quantock Hills about ten miles west of Bridgwater. On the 13th of June, Charles replied to Coleridge's invitation to pay him a visit. "You press me, very kindly do you press me, to come to Stowey," he wrote. "Obstacles strong as death, prevent me at present; maybe I may be able to come before the year is out. Believe me, I will come as soon as I can; but I dread naming a probable time. It depends on fifty things, besides the expense, which is not nothing."

In the meantime, Mary had sufficiently recovered her sanity for her to be allowed to leave the asylum (under the supervision of a nurse or attendant), and to be moved by Charles into lodgings at Hackney, where he visited her every Sunday, and in any other spare moments that he could find. "She boards herself," he told Coleridge. "In a little half-year's illness, of such a nature, and of such consequences, to get her out into the world again, and with a prospect of her never being so ill again, – this is to be ranked not among the common blessings of Providence. May that merciful God make tender my heart, and make me as thankful, as in my distress I was earnest, in my prayers. Congratulate me on an ever-present and never alienable friend like her."

Far from waiting until the end of the year to venture into the West Country, we find Charles at Nether Stowey by the beginning of July. Coleridge, in fact, had only recently returned home after spending three deliriously happy weeks with William and Dorothy Wordsworth, both of whom he was meeting for the first time. The brother and sister, both of whom were natives of Cockermouth, were living at Racedown Lodge in Dorset; a three-storey Georgian house near the village of Bettiscombe, about forty miles from Nether Stowey. William Wordsworth and Coleridge spent much of the time reading aloud each other's work, and generally revelling in each other's company. The three of them quickly became such good friends, in fact, that the Wordsworths were easily persuaded by Coleridge to join him on his return to the domestic hearth. Not long after they were all ensconced in the tiny, cramped cottage, Charles arrived from London to swell the party still further. The Wordsworths never did return to Racedown Lodge after this first visit; Coleridge found them a property – Alfoxden House – which was only four miles distant from Nether Stowey and available to rent immediately. Henceforth, they could enjoy as much of each other's company as they wished. In her *Alfoxden Journal*, Dorothy wrote: "There is everything here; sea, woods wild as fancy ever painted, brooks clear and pebbly as in Cumberland, villages so romantic, [but] our principal inducement was Coleridge's society."

It was at this time that William Wordsworth and Coleridge collaborated on their volume *Lyrical Ballads* published in 1798. The collection opened with Coleridge's *The Rime of the Ancient Mariner* and closed with Wordsworth's *Lines Written Above Tintern Abbey*. There were twenty-four poems altogether, nineteen of which were composed by Wordsworth. A prepublication advertisement declared that the book would offer 'a natural delineation of human passions, human characters and human incidents'. Although *Lyrical Ballads* received a cool reception from the critics and public alike when it first appeared, "over the course of years", wrote Ackroyd in his *History of England* (Volume IV, 2016), "it became the source and fountain of what became known as the Romantic sensibility of the early nineteenth century in England, part of a movement of taste which stretched across France and Germany, Russia and Italy and Spain".

The week that Charles spent at Nether Stowey was filled with people, lively conversation and local excursions. It was a great contrast to his drab life at home waiting upon his ailing father. Coleridge was unable to join his friends on one of their walks, owing to a slight leg injury which confined him to the garden. Disappointed not to be making up one of the party and swathed in self-pity, he employed the time while his visitors were out enjoying themselves by composing a poem, *This Lime-Tree Bower my Prison*:

...Yes! They wander on
In gladness all; but thou, methinks, most glad,
My gentle-hearted Charles! For thou hast pined
And hungered after Nature, many a year,
In the great City pent, winning thy way
With sad yet patient soul, through evil and pain
And strange calamity!...

Coleridge addressed his old schoolfriend as 'My gentle-hearted Charles' several times in these lines. When the poem was subsequently published in the *Annual Anthology* of 1800 (a publication brought out by Joseph Cottle, a Bristol bookseller, jointly with Coleridge and Southey), Charles rounded on its author. "For God's sake (I was never more serious), don't make me ridiculous any more by terming me gentle-hearted in print, or do it in better verses. It did well enough [three] years ago when I came to see you and was moral coxcomb enough at the time you wrote the lines, to feed upon such epithets; but, besides that, the meaning of gentle is equivocal at best, and almost always means poor-spirited, the very quality of gentleness is abhorrent to such vile trumpetings... I can scarce think but you meant it in joke. I hope you did, for I should be ashamed to think that you could think to gratify me by such praise, fit only to be a cordial to some green-sick sonneteer... In the next edition of the 'Anthology'... please to blot out 'gentle-hearted' and substitute drunken, dog, ragged-head, seld-shaven, odd-eyed, stuttering, or any other epithet which truly and properly belongs to the gentleman in question."

The biographer, Edith Christina Johnson, in *Lamb Always Elia* (1935), settled for "the stout-hearted, the magnanimous, the unconquerable, and the irresistible Charles Lamb".

Undeniably, Charles thoroughly enjoyed his visit to Nether Stowey, while still not being quite at his ease in the company of people – such as the Wordsworths – who had been hitherto unknown to him. Then, on arriving home, he discovered that he had left his great-coat behind, "in the oblivious state the mind is thrown into at parting", and immediately wrote asking Coleridge to "…send it to me by a Stowey waggon [sic], if there be such a thing. Is it not ridiculous that I sometimes envy that great-coat lingering so cunningly behind! …I could not talk much while I was with you; but my silence was not sullenness, nor I hope from any bad motive; but, in truth, disuse has made me awkward at it. I know I behaved myself, particularly at Tom Poole's, and at Cruikshank's… but company and converse are strange to me. It was kind in you all to endure me as you did".

***

The start of 1798 saw Mary in the throes of a relapse, one which required her return to an asylum. It would seem that Coleridge suggested she might stay at Nether Stowey once she had recovered, for a period of recuperation. Charles's response on the 28th of January was unequivocal. "Your invitation went to my very heart; but you have a power of exciting interest, of leading all hearts captive, too forcible to admit of Mary's being with you. I consider her as permanently on the brink of madness. I think you would almost make her dance within an inch of the precipice; she must be with duller fancies and cooler intellects. I know a young man of this description, who has suited her these twenty years, and may live to do so still, if we are one day restored to each other."

During the course of the year, in the precious spare moments that were left to him in between work, caring for his ailing father and visiting Mary in her lodgings, Charles managed to write a short novel, in which he drew upon his childhood recollections of Widford and Blakesware for its background scenes. The eponymous heroine lives with her elderly grandmother in a small cottage close to the large, old house, and the slight tale is played out in those surroundings that were so familiar to its author. He summons up the old mansion with a palpable air of nostalgia. "Our old house was vacant and to be sold. I entered unmolested, into the room that had been my bed-chamber. I kneeled down on the spot where my little bed had stood – I felt like a child – I prayed like one – it seemed as though old times were to return again – I looked round involuntarily, expecting to see some face I knew – but… the bed was gone. My little pane of painted window, through which I loved to look at the sun, when I awoke on a fine summer's morning, was taken out, and had been replaced by one of common glass.

"I visited by turns every chamber: they were all desolate and unfurnished, one excepted, in which the owner had left a harpsichord, probably to be sold. I touched the keys. I played some old Scottish tunes, which had delighted me when a child. Past associations revived with the music, blended with a sense of unreality, which at last became too powerful. I rushed out of the room to give vent to my feelings."

By any reckoning, *Rosamund Gray* was a thin tale and decidedly melodramatic. It was never destined to become a classic. "Not quite convincing" was how Lucas described it. "But its quality is of the rarest. The early chapters have an extraordinary charm of simplicity; the later, a curious and painful intensity of feeling."

***

As Claudius laments in Shakespeare's *Hamlet*, "When sorrows come, they come not single spies/But in battalions", and Charles had a further two waves of grief to crest during the course of the next few years. In April 1799, his father died after several years of declining health; a decline which seems to have begun as early as 1792, following the death of Salt; at which time John Lamb Senior would have been in his mid-fifties. Southey records that, when he saw Charles's father during the winter of 1794–95, "When I saw the family (one evening only) they... were evidently in uncomfortable circumstances. The father and mother were both living; and I have some dim recollection of the latter's invalid appearance. The father's senses had failed him before that time. He published some poems in quarto. Lamb showed me once an imperfect copy: *The Sparrow's Wedding* was the title of the longest piece, and this was the author's favourite; he liked, in his dotage, to hear Charles read it".

It is possible to glean something of John Lamb's last days from the son's thinly veiled account of his father (as Lovel) in *The Old Benchers of the Inner Temple*. "I saw him in his old age, and the decay of his faculties, palsy-smitten in the last sad stage of human weakness – a remnant most forlorn of what he was! – yet even then his eyes would light up upon the mention of his favourite Garrick... And then, the excitement subsiding, he would weep, till I have wished that sad second childhood might have a mother still to lay its head upon her lap. But the common mother of us all in no long time after received him gently into hers." John Lamb was buried on the 13th of April 1799 at St. James's Church, Clerkenwell, which was also Aunt Hetty's final resting place.

After their father's death, Mary Lamb was able to return to the family home to be cared for by her younger brother, who was now aged twenty-four. Before this was possible, however, Charles was required to give "his solemn engagement that he would take her under his care for life". It was a promise that he adhered to most faithfully, and one that he honoured until the day he died.

By the time that Mary was allowed to join him at home, Charles had moved just a few houses along the same road to

35 Chapel Street. Sadly, any hopes he had once entertained that Mary would experience no relapses of her illness were well and truly dispelled by now. One friend, Bryan Waller Proctor, who practised as a solicitor and published his memoir of Charles in 1866 (using his pen name Barry Cornwall) recalled, when writing of this period in their lives at Pentonville, that "whenever the approach of one of Mary's fits of insanity was announced, by some irritability or change of manner, Lamb would take her, under his arm, to Hoxton Asylum. It was very affecting to encounter the young brother and his sister walking together (weeping together) on this painful errand; Mary herself, although sad, very conscious of the necessity for temporary separation from her only friend. They used to carry a straight-jacket with them".

In the early summer of 1800, Charles and Mary decided to move back to lodgings in the centre of town, residing for a while at Southampton Buildings in Chancery Lane, Holborn. Before leaving Pentonville, however, Charles wrote on the 17th of March to a recently acquired friend, Thomas Manning, who was a mathematics tutor at Cambridge. He was also a noted sinologist, and the first Englishman ever to enter Lhasa, the holy city of Tibet. "I am living in a continuous feast," Charles wrote. "Coleridge has been with me now for nigh three weeks, and the more I see of him… the more cause I see to love him, and believe him a very good man, and all those foolish impressions to the contrary fly off like morning slumbers. He is engaged in translations, which I hope will keep him this month to come. He is uncommonly kind and friendly to me. He ferrets me day and night to DO SOMETHING. He tends me, amidst all his own worrying and heart-oppressing occupations, as a gardener tends his young tulip… He has lugged me to the brink of engaging to a newspaper, and has suggested to me, for a first plan, the forgery of a supposed manuscript of [Robert] Burton, the anatomist of melancholy. I have even written the introductory letter; and if I can pick up a few guineas this way, I feel they will be most refreshing, bread being so dear. If I go on with it, I will apprise you of it, as you may like to see my things! And the tulip, of all flowers, loves to be admired most."

Less than two months later, Charles told Coleridge that, "I don't know why I write [to you], except from the propensity which misery has to tell her griefs. Hetty [Charles and Mary's servant], died on Friday night, about eleven o'clock, after eight days' illness. Mary, in consequence of fatigue and anxiety, is fallen ill again, and I was obliged to remove her yesterday. I am left alone in a house with nothing but Hetty's dead body to keep me company. Tomorrow I bury her, and then I shall be quite alone, with nothing but a cat to remind me that the house has been full of living beings like myself. My heart is quite sunk, and I don't know where to look for relief".

Chapter Five

A 'Double Singleness'

King's Bench Walk, The Temple.

From the moment that Charles and Mary set up home together at 36 Chapel Street, they lived from that time forward in what Charles described as "a sort of double singleness", until death eventually separated them. It was a way of life, as Martin wrote, "that was consoled by their mutual affection, cheered by their common tastes [and] brightened by the companionship of congenial beings". An affecting vignette of what their life together might have been like during their earliest days of shared adult domesticity, when they were not so comfortably fixed as later on, is provided by Charles in his Elia essay, *Old China* (1823), in which 'Bridget Elia' [Mary] reflects upon those times "when we were not quite so rich. I do not mean that I want to be poor; but there was a middle state… in which I am sure we were a great deal happier. [Not that Charles and Mary were ever rich, but they did eventually become 'comfortable'.] A purchase is but a purchase, now that you have money enough and to spare. Formerly it used to be a triumph. When we coveted a cheap luxury… we were used to have a debate two or three days before, and to weigh the for and against, and think what we might spare it out of, and what saving we could hit upon that should be an equivalent. A thing was worth buying then, when we felt the money that we paid for it.

"Do you remember the brown suit, which you made to hang upon you, till all your friends cried in shame upon you, it grew so threadbare, and all because of that folio Beaumont and Fletcher, which you dragged home late at night from Barker's in Covent Garden? Do you remember how we eyed it for weeks before we could make up our minds to the purchase, and had not come to a determination till it was near ten o'clock of the Saturday night, when you set off… fearing you should be too late… Then do you remember our pleasant walks to Enfield, and Potter's Bar and Waltham, when we had a holiday… and the little hand-basket in which I used to deposit our day's fare of savoury cold lamb and salad – and how you would pry about at noontide for some decent house, where we might go in and produce our store – only paying for the ale that you must call for – and speculate upon the looks of the landlady, and whether she was likely to allow us a table-cloth – and wish for such another honest hostess as Izaak

Walton has described many a one on the pleasant banks of the Lea when he went a-fishing – and sometimes they would prove obliging enough, and sometimes they would look grudgingly upon us – but we had cheerful looks still for one another, and would eat our plain food savourily... Now, when we go out a day's pleasuring, which is seldom moreover, we ride part of the way – and go into a fine inn, and order the best of dinners, never debating the expense – which, after all, never has half the relish of those chance country snaps, when we were at the mercy of uncertain usage, and a precarious welcome".

***

For Charles, living in the little house at Pentonville felt increasingly like being sent into exile. In particular, he missed his friends, even those of whom he sometimes complained that their – usually uninvited – visits deprived him of his concentration and the solitude he craved in order to be able to write. Sadly, it was also a fact that Mary's tragic history followed her (and therefore Charles, too), wherever she went. "We are in a manner 'marked'," he told Coleridge. "Nor is it the least of our evils that her case and all our story is so well known around us." It is probable that their neighbours at Pentonville sometimes looked askance at the brother and sister as they went about their daily affairs, making the pair of them feel conspicuous or even slightly uneasy in the process.

"I have had a very eligible offer to lodge with a friend in town," Charles told Manning. "He will have rooms to let at midsummer [1800]... It is a great object to me to live in town, where we shall be much more private. We can be nowhere private except in the midst of London."

The friend in question was John Matthew Gutch, a Christ's Hospital schoolfellow of both Coleridge and Charles.

"Soon after I wrote to you last, an offer was made me by Gutch (you must remember him at Christ's)… to come and lodge with him at his house in Southampton Buildings, Chancery Lane [where he ran a stationer's business]," Charles told Coleridge later in the summer. "This was a very comfortable offer to me, the rooms being at a reasonable rent, and including the use of an old servant, besides being infinitely preferable to ordinary lodgings in our case, as you must perceive. As Gutch knew all our story and the perpetual liability to a recurrence in my sister's disorder, probably to the end of her life, I certainly think the offer very generous and very friendly. I have got three rooms, (including servant) under £34 a year. Here I soon found myself at home; and here, in six weeks after, Mary was well enough to join me. So we are once more settled. I am afraid we are not placed out of the reach of future interruptions. But I am determined to take what snatches of pleasure we can between the acts of our distressful drama."

Mitre Court Buildings, The Temple.

Charles was delighted that he had returned to 'town', as he put it; which in itself suggests how comparatively rural he regarded Pentonville in relation to Southampton Buildings. However, the arrangement with Gutch was destined not to last long. In the early spring of 1801, Charles informed Manning that he was going to change his lodgings once again, "having received a hint that it would be agreeable, at Our Lady's next feast [the 25th of March]. I have partly fixed upon the most delectable rooms, which look out (when you stand on tiptoe) over the Thames and Surrey Hills; at the upper end of King's Bench Walk in the Temple. There I shall have all the privacy of a house without the encumbrance, and shall be able to lock my friends out as often as I desire to hold free converse with my immortal mind; for my present lodgings resemble a minister's levee, I have so increased my acquaintance (as they call 'em) since I have resided in town. Like the country mouse, that had tasted a little of urbane manners, I long to be nibbling my own cheese by my dear self, without mouse-traps and time-traps. By my new plan, I shall be as airy, up four pair of stairs, as in the country; and in a garden, in the midst of enchanting… London, whose dirtiest drab-frequented alley, and her lowest bowing tradesmen, I would not exchange for Skiddaw, Helvellyn… and the parson into the bargain."

In April, Charles wrote again to Manning, announcing that, "I live at 16 Mitre Court Buildings, a pistol-shot off Baron Maseres'… [A man of many parts: distinguished lawyer, judge, and one-time Governor of the Canadian province of Quebec.] You must introduce me to the Baron. I think we should suit one another mainly. He lives on the ground floor, for convenience of the gout; I prefer the attic story [sic], for the air. He keeps three footmen and two maids; I have neither maid nor laundress, not caring to be troubled with them. His forte, I understand, is the higher mathematics; my turn, I confess, is more to poetry and the belles lettres. The very antithesis of our characters would make up a harmony. You must bring the Baron and me together. When you come to see me, mount up to the top of the stairs – I hope you are not asthmatical – and come in flannel, for 'tis pure airy up there. And bring your glass, and I will show you the Surrey Hills. My bed faces the river, so as by perking up upon my haunches, and supporting my carcass with my elbows, without much wrying my neck, I can see the white sails glide by the bottom of the King's Bench Walk as I lie in my bed. An excellent tiptoe prospect in the best room: casement windows, with small panes, to look more like a cottage".

His sheer delight in returning to his beloved Temple is palpable, and Charles and Mary were to remain at Mitre Court Buildings until 1809. (The actual building inhabited by the Lambs has been subsequently demolished – like so much of the London with which they were familiar- but a later structure of the same name occupies the site.)

Charles wrote an illuminating essay that appeared in his friend James Leigh Hunt's journal, *Reflector*, in February 1802, in which he attempted to explain the magnetic pull which his native city exerted over him. "…I consider myself in some sort a speculative Lord Mayor of London: for though circumstances unhappily preclude me from the hope of ever arriving at the dignity of a gold chain… yet thus much I will say of myself in truth that Whittington with his Cat (just emblem of vigilance and a furred gown) never went beyond me in affection, which I bear to the citizens. I was born… in a crowd. This has begot in me an entire affection for that way of life, amounting to an almost insurmountable aversion from solitude and rural scenes. This aversion was never interrupted, or suspended, except for a few years in the younger part of my life, during a period in which I had set my affections upon a charming young woman.

Every man while the passion is upon him is for a time at least addicted to groves and meadows and purling streams. During this short period of my existence, I contracted just familiarity enough with rural objects to understand tolerably well ever after the poets, when they declaim in such passionate terms in favour of a country life.

"For my part, now the fit is past, I have no hesitation in declaring, that a mob of happy faces crowding up at the pit-door of Drury-lane Theatre, just at the hour of six, gives me ten thousand sincerer pleasures, than I could ever receive from all the flocks of silly sheep that ever whitened the plains of Arcadia or Epsom Downs.

"I am naturally inclined to hypochondria, but in London it vanishes, like all other ills. Often, when I have felt a weariness or distaste at home, have I rushed out into her crowded Strand, and fed my humour till tears have wetted my cheek for inutterable sympathies with the multitudinous moving picture, which she never fails to present at all hours, like the scenes of a shifting pantomime... I love the very smoke of London, because it has been the medium most familiar to my vision. I see grand principles of honour at work in the dirty ring which encompasses two combatants with fists, and principles of no less eternal justice in the detection of a pickpocket. The salutary astonishment with which an execution is surveyed, convinces me more forcibly than a hundred volumes of abstract polity, that the universal instinct of man in all ages has leaned to order and good government.

"Thus an art of extracting morality from the commonest incidents of a town life, is attained by the same well-natured alchemy, with which the Foresters of Arden, in a beautiful country, 'Found tongues in trees, books in the running brooks, Sermons in stones, and good in every thing'."

Charles was still only twenty-six (Mary was in her mid-thirties) when they returned to live in the Temple. By this time, Charles had attracted and gathered around him an impressive and varied collection of friends which, of course, included Coleridge above all, the Wordsworths and Southey. The poet and critic George Dyer and the philosopher and novelist William Godwin were also among the better-known of Charles's intimates. Many years later, Charles wrote of himself that he chose his companions "for some individuality of character which they manifested. – Hence, not many persons of science, and few professed literati, were of his councils. They were, for the most part, persons of an uncertain fortune. – His intimados, to confess a truth, were in the world's eye a ragged regiment. He found them floating on the surface of society; and the colour, or something else, in the weed pleased him. The burrs stuck to him – but they were good and loving burrs for all that. He never greatly cared for the society of what are called good people".

***

Shortly after returning from his visit to Coleridge at Nether Stowey during the summer of 1797, Charles – despite the tragedy and turmoil of so many months past – set to work on what he described as a dramatic poem, *John Woodvil: A Tragedy*. (His novel *Rosamund Gray* had been written around the same time and, as we have seen, appeared the following year.) "My Tragedy will be a medley… of laughter and tears, prose and verse, and in some places rhyme, songs, wit, pathos, humour, and, if possible, sublimity," he told Southey in November 1798. "At least it is not a fault in my intention, if it does not comprehend most of these discordant colours. Heaven send they dance not the 'Dance of Death.'"

Unfortunately, they did! *John Woodvil* was eventually printed and published in February 1802 at Charles's own expense but was poorly received by the critics. Southey thought it was 'lukewarm', for example, and the *Annual Review* declared it to be "…precious nonsense! But this is a specimen of that canting, whining style, or rather 'slang' of poetry, which is nowadays offered to us as the very essence of simplicity and pathos!". The writer of this unfriendly review was believed (erroneously, as it subsequently turned out) to have been Mrs. Barbauld, an authoress of the day. Before she had been discovered entirely innocent in the matter, however, Southey fired off this letter to Coleridge: "Why have you not made Lamb declare war upon Mrs. Barbauld? He should singe her flaxen wig with squibs, and tie crackers to her petticoats till she leaped about like a parched pea for very torture. There is not a man in the world who could so well revenge himself."

Any hopes Charles had entertained that the piece might be produced on the professional stage at Drury Lane were not fulfilled.

However, putting to one side the disappointment he may have felt over the failure of *John Woodvil*, Charles used his annual leave from the East India House during the summer of 1802 on what was, for him, an uncharacteristic and quite reckless adventure. Without even sending word in advance that they were on their way, Charles and Mary left London in early August, and made the long and arduous journey by mail coach to Keswick in Cumberland. Coleridge had moved to Greta Hall where, once again, he could be close to the Wordsworths, who were now settled fifteen miles to the south at Grasmere. Charles had firmly rejected the idea of visiting Wordsworth at the beginning of the previous year. "I ought before this to have replied to your very kind invitation into Cumberland," he had written to William on the 30th of January 1801. "With you and your sister I could gang anywhere; but I am afraid whether I shall ever be able to afford so desperate a journey. Separate from the pleasure of your company, I don't much care if I never see a mountain in my life. I have passed all my days in London… my attachments are all purely local." But now he had been tempted to visit the Lake District at last.

Originally built as an astronomical observatory, Greta Hall had been refashioned by the beginning of the nineteenth century as a three storey-high squire's country house, with just a hint of the observatory remaining. As Richard Holmes vividly describes it in *Coleridge: Early Visions* (1989), "To this day, its white facade can be seen shining out of Keswick from almost every peak of the encircling fells – most impressively perhaps from Cat Bells across Derwent Water – a sort of landlocked lighthouse, upon which the lonely fell-walker can always get an accurate compass fix in his wanderings."

Arriving at Greta Hall completely unheralded, Charles and Mary were fortunate to find their friend at home, after a 250-mile expedition of several days' duration. "I set out with Mary to Keswick, without giving Coleridge any notice, for my time being precious did not admit of it," Charles wrote to Manning on the 24th of September, in a long and detailed account of his Lake District adventures. "He received us with all the hospitality in the world, and gave up his time to show us all the wonders of the country. He dwells upon a small hill by the side of Keswick, in a comfortable house, quite enveloped on all sides by a net of mountains; great floundering bears and monsters they seemed, all couchant and asleep. We got in in the evening, travelling in a post-chaise from Penrith, in the midst of a gorgeous sunshine, which transmuted all the mountains into colours, purple, etc. etc. We thought we had got into fairyland. But that went off (as it never came again; while we stayed we had no more fine sunsets), and we entered Coleridge's comfortable study just in the dusk, when the mountains were all dark with clouds upon their heads. Such an impression I never received from objects of sight before, nor do I suppose I can ever again. Glorious creatures, fine old fellows, Skiddaw etc. I shall never forget ye, how ye lay about that night, like an entrenchment; gone to bed, as it seemed for the night, but promising that ye were to be seen in the morning. Coleridge had got a blazing fire in his study; which is a large antique, ill-shaped room, with an old-fashioned organ, never played upon, big enough for a church, shelves of scattered folios, an Aeolian harp, and an old sofa, half bed etc. And all looking out upon the last fading view of Skiddaw, and his broad-breasted brethren: what a night!"

Charles and Mary stayed in the Lakes for three weeks and, allowing for the travelling time involved at each end of their journey, they were away from home for a month in total. During this time they paid a visit to the Wordsworths at Dove Cottage (a former inn known as the Dove and Olive Branch). On this occasion, however, their unplanned arrival did not pay off: William and Dorothy were away from home, on holiday in Calais. "We have seen Keswick, Grasmere, Ambleside, Ullswater, and a place at the other end of Ullswater; I forget the name; to which we travelled on a very sultry day, over the middle of Helvellyn," Charles informed Manning. "We have clambered up to the top of Skiddaw, and I have waded up the bed of Lodore. In fine, I have satisfied myself that there is such a thing as that which tourists call 'romantic', which I very much suspected before; they make such a spluttering about it, and toss their splendid epithets around them, till they give as dim a light as at four o'clock next morning the lamps do after an illumination. Mary was excessively tired when she got about halfway up Skiddaw, but we came to a cold rill (than which nothing can be imagined more cold, running over cold stones), and with the reinforcement of a draught of cold water she surmounted it most manfully. Oh, its fine black head, and the bleak air atop of it, with a prospect of mountains all about and about, making you giddy; and then Scotland afar off [on the northern side of the Solway Firth], and the border countries so famous in song and ballad! It was a day that will stand out, like a mountain, I am sure, in my life. But I am returned (I have now been come home near three weeks) and you cannot conceive the degredation I felt at first, from being accustomed to wander free as air among mountains, and bathe in rivers without being controlled by anyone, to come home and work."

Following his return to London, Charles also wrote to Coleridge (somewhat melodramatically) that, "I feel I shall remember your mountains to the last day of my life. They haunt me perpetually. I am like a man who has been falling in love unknown to himself, which he finds out when he leaves the lady". However, the native Londoner within Charles surfaced before long. "But that is going off," he told Manning, "and I find I shall conform in time to that state of life to which it has pleased God to call me. Besides, after all, Fleet Street and the Strand are better places to live in for good and all than amidst SKIDDAW… After all, I could not LIVE in Skiddaw. I could spend a year, two, three years among [the fells], but I must have a prospect of seeing Fleet Street at the end of that time, or I should mope and pine away, I know. Still, Skiddaw is a fine creature."

***

The year 1804 marked the beginning of a significant new friendship in Charles's life. William Hazlitt, born in 1778 as the son of a Unitarian minister, initially tried to make his living as a portrait painter. However, after being encouraged to write by his friend Coleridge, he subsequently became a prolific essayist and, in 1825, published *The Spirit of the Age*. The book comprised a collection of essays in which Hazlitt provided descriptive character sketches – and analysed the writing – of such contemporaries as Wordsworth, Coleridge and Lamb. The work represented arguably Hazlitt's finest achievement as a writer and critic. According to Hazlitt's own account, his first meeting with Charles took place at the house of the philosopher, novelist, and author of *Political Justice* (1793), William Godwin. Hazlitt's famous portrait of Charles (aged thirty and somewhat incongruously dressed as a Venetian Senator), which hangs in the National Portrait Gallery in London, is one of the last paintings he executed.

For a portrait of a different kind, however, we can turn to a young Thomas De Quincey. Best known today, perhaps, for his *Confessions of an English Opium-Eater* (1822), he became a friend of the Lake Poets, and worked as a prodigiously industrious freelance journalist throughout his ramshackle and debt-ridden life. The year in question was either late 1804 or early 1805 (De Quincey was then only nineteen), when he gathered the impressions for this description of Charles at his place of work. The resulting essay was not published until 1838, in *Tait's Edinburgh Magazine.* He captured a scene that would have varied little over the course of the many thousands of such days that Charles occupied his desk in Leadenhall Street. Armed with a letter of introduction from a mutual literary friend, De Quincey "…went to the India House, made enquiries among the servants and, after some trouble (for that was early in his Leadenhall Street career, and possibly he was not much known), I was shown into a small room, or else a small section of a large one, in which was a very lofty writing-desk, separated by a still-higher railing from that part of the floor on which the profane – the laity, like myself – were allowed to approach the clerkly rulers of the room. Within the railing sat, to the best of my remembrance, six quill-driving gentlemen; not gentlemen whose duty or profession it was merely to drive the quill but who were then driving it in act as well as habit; for, as if they supposed me a spy sent by some superior power to report upon the situation of affairs as surprised by me, they were all too profoundly immersed in their oriental studies to have any sense of my presence. Consequently, I was reduced to the necessity of announcing myself and my errand. I walked, therefore, into one of the two open doorways of the railing, and stood closely by the high stool of him who occupied the first place within the little aisle. I touched his arm, by way of recalling him from his lofty Leadenhall speculations to this sublunary world; and, presenting my letter asked if that gentleman were really a citizen of the present room; for I had been repeatedly misled, by the directions given me, into wrong rooms. The gentleman smiled; it was a smile not to be forgotten. This was Lamb… The letter of introduction, containing (I imagine) no matters of business, was speedily run through; and I instantly received an invitation to spend the evening with him. Lamb was not one of those who catch at the chance of escaping from a bore by fixing some distant day, when accidents may have carried you away from the place: he sought to benefit by no luck of that kind; for he was, with his limited income, positively the most hospitable man I have known in this world. That night, the same night, I was to come and spend the evening with him. I had gone to the India House with the express purpose of accepting whatever invitation he should give me; and therefore, I accepted this, took my leave, and left Lamb in the act of resuming his aerial position."

That evening, De Quincey met Mary for the first time, "of whom, and whose talents and sweetness of disposition I had heard". Nothing about the even tenor of Charles's life at his office or the harmonious atmosphere of that evening at the

Temple, would have given De Quincey any idea of the emotional and domestic turmoil into which Charles's life was periodically thrown at the hands of his sister's recurring bouts of insanity. Only a few months after De Quincey's visit to the East India House, Charles was unburdening himself on the subject to Dorothy Wordsworth, in a letter, dated the 14th of June: "[Mary] has been attacked by one of her severe illnesses, and is at present from home. Last Monday week is the day she left me, and I hope I may calculate upon having her again in a month or a little more. When she discovers symptoms of approaching illness, it is not easy to say what is best to do. Being by ourselves is bad, and going out is bad. I get so irritable and wretched with fear, that I constantly hasten on the disorder. You cannot conceive the misery of such a foresight. I am sure that, for the week before she left me, I was little better than light-headed… I have every reason to suppose that this illness, like all her former ones, will be but temporary but… meantime she is dead to me and I miss a prop. She lives but for me."

***

It was at 16 Mitre Court Buildings, in 1806, that Charles and Mary's famous Wednesday evening gatherings were initiated. (Later on they were moved to Thursdays.) Writing to Manning (who had sailed for China earlier that year), in a letter dated the 5th of December, Charles explained – with his tongue firmly in his cheek – that, "like other great men, I have a public day, cribbage and pipes…". He goes on to describe his new play, a farce in two acts, which was due to be put on at Drury Lane. "The title is '*Mr. H.*', no more. How simple. How taking! A great H sprawling over the playbill and attracting eyes at every corner. The story is a coxcomb appearing at Bath, vastly rich – all the ladies dying for him – all bursting to know who he is; but he

A 'Double Singleness'

goes by no other name than *'Mr. H.'* ...I shall get £200 from the theatre if *'Mr. H.'* has a good run, and I hope £100 for the copyright. Nothing if it fails; and there never was a more ticklish thing."

Sadly, the play was hissed at by the audience when it was produced a few nights later on the 10th of December (although Charles reported that the prologue "went splendidly"), and the performance was not repeated. Subsequently, however, the play was well-received in the United States. Charles wrote to Wordsworth the following day, informing him that, "*'Mr. H.'* came out last night, and failed. I had many fears; the subject was not substantial enough... We are pretty stout about it; have had plenty of condoling friends; but, after all, we had rather it should have succeeded. You will see the prologue in most of the morning papers. It was received with such shouts as I never witnessed to a prologue. It was attempted to be encored. How hard! – a thing I did merely as a task, because it was wanted, and set no great store by; and *'Mr. H.'*!!! The number of friends we had in the house – my brother and I being in public offices etc. – was astonishing, but they yielded at length to a few hisses. A hundred hisses! ...A hundred hisses outweigh a thousand claps. The former come more directly from the heart. Well, 'tis withdrawn, and there is an end."

Charles confessed that he joined in with audience's hisses himself "because he was so damnably afraid of being taken for the author". Although he seems to have borne this unequivocal failure in good part, it must have been a crushing personal blow to him at the time, not least because he had spent a whole year working on the play.

Within just a month or so of this disappointment, however, Charles published his *Tales from Shakespeare*. It appeared in January 1807, as a title in Godwin's *Juvenile Library* series of books. It consisted of a collection of essays written in collaboration with

Mary and intended "for the use of young persons". They were, in effect, a retelling of the bard's tragedies and comedies (the histories were not included), couched in a narrative style that children could easily comprehend, while retaining as much of Shakespeare's original language, imagery and spirit as was compatible with the enterprise. Charles tackled the tragedies, and Mary applied herself to the comedies. The true purpose of this work, however, shines out in the closing paragraph of the authors' joint preface to it. "What these Tales shall have been to the young readers, that and much more it is the writers' wish that the true Plays of Shakespeare may prove to them in older years – enrichers of the fancy, strengtheners of virtue, a withdrawing from all selfish and mercenary thoughts, a lesson of all sweet and honourable thoughts and actions, to teach courtesy, benignity, generosity, humanity: for of examples, teaching these virtues, his pages are full."

Writing to her friend (and Hazlitt's future wife) Sarah Stoddart, on the 2nd of June 1806, Mary described the method of working together that she and Charles employed. "You would like to see us, as we often sit, writing on one table (but not on one cushion sitting), like Hermia and Helena in the *Midsummer Night's Dream*; or, rather, like an old literary Darby and Joan; I taking snuff, and he groaning all the while and saying he can make nothing of it, which he always says till he has finished, and then he finds out he has made something of it…".

There were occasions when Mary also found the work difficult. "Mary is just stuck fast in *All's Well that Ends Well*," Charles confided in a letter to Wordsworth, a few weeks later. "She complains of having to set forth so many female characters in boy's clothes. I, to encourage her, for she often faints in the prosecution of her great work, flatter her with telling her how well such a play and such a play is done. But she is stuck fast, and I have been obliged to promise to assist her."

Tales from Shakespeare was originally published without

the final 'e' in the title. The book has been reprinted, and new editions issued countless times over the years. It remains in print to this day and has been translated into approximately forty different languages.

During 1808, Charles wrote (without Mary's assistance on this occasion) and published *The Adventures of Ulysses* which was, again, intended for the enjoyment of young people. More significantly, however, he also published during the summer of that year his *Specimens of English Dramatic Poets who lived about the Time of Shakespeare*. "The work," declared Lucas, which Charles had been tinkering with sporadically over a long period, "laid the foundation of his reputation as a critic. Until its appearance he had been known, if at all, only as an experimentalist in verse, prose, and the drama. But to the discerning eye there was nothing tentative about the notes and selections in this new volume; they were the work of an imaginative critic of a very high order, who knew his own mind."

Canon Alfred Ainger, when assessing Charles's contribution as a literary critic in *Lamb* (1882), believed that, "If it is too much to say that he singly revived the sixteenth and seventeenth centuries, it is because we see clearly that that revival was coming, and would have come even without his help. But he did more than recall attention to certain forgotten writers. He flashed a light from himself upon them, not only heightening every charm and deepening every truth, but making even their eccentricities beautiful and lovable. And in doing this he has linked his name for ever with theirs. When we think of… [Christopher] Marlowe, [Michael] Drayton, Drummond of Hawthornden and [Abraham] Cowley, then the thought of Charles Lamb will never be far off". Charles himself declared that his purpose had been to show "how much of Shakespeare shines in the great men his contemporaries, and how far in his divine mind and manners he surpassed them and all mankind".

The end of 1808 (although the book was dated 1809) saw the publication of a second joint collection of essays for young people written by Charles and Mary, bearing the cumbersome title of *Mrs. Leicester's School; or The History of Several Young Ladies Related by Themselves*. On this occasion, Mary contributed the lion's share of the stories (seven out of the ten were written by her, and three by Charles) and, although it has not endured in the same way as *Tales from Shakespeare*, the volume was well-regarded in its day. Several of Mary's stories hark back to the days of her childhood visits to Hertfordshire. *Louisa Manners; or The Farm House* evokes impressions of Mackery End which, in Mary's tale, "stood all alone by itself, no house to be seen at all near it". *Margaret Green, or The Young Mahometan*, on the other hand, conjures up childhood visits to Blakesware. Margaret's mother was companion to a rich elderly lady who lived alone in the old family mansion. The young girl was allowed to wander all over the house at will, and in due course came upon the existence of an impressively large library; such a collection of books, in fact, as to rival that of Salt's in his Temple chambers. "This was indeed a precious discovery," Margaret declared. "If you never spent whole mornings alone in a large library, you cannot conceive the pleasure of taking down books in the constant hope of finding an entertaining book among them; yet, after many days, meeting with nothing but disappointment, it becomes less pleasant. All the books within my reach were folios of the gravest cast. I could understand very little that I read in them, and the old dark print and the length of the lines made my eyes ache."

Assessing the impact of *Mrs. Leicester's School* a century after it first appeared, Lucas wrote that "it has never had the favour it deserved and probably now [1905] never will. Its old-fashioned and rather formal machinery has perhaps been against it; but those who love the stories love them exceedingly".

Chapter Six

'Transplanted from Our Native Soil'

Button Snap. (Date and source unknown.)

After living for eight years at 16 Mitre Court Buildings, Charles and Mary were obliged to 'up sticks' and move once again, as their landlord needed the rooms they occupied for his own use. They were fortunate in soon finding another set of chambers in the Temple which were available to rent, as Charles informed Manning in a letter dated the 28th of March 1809. "Don't come any more to Mitre Court Buildings," he commanded. (In fact, Manning was hardly likely to call on the off chance, given that he was living in China at this time!) "We are at 34 Southampton Buildings, Chancery Lane, and shall be here until about the end of May; then we remove to No. 4 Inner Temple Lane, where I mean to live and die, for I have such a horror of moving... What a dislocation of comfort is comprised in that word 'moving'!

"Such a heap of little nasty things, after you think all is got into the cart: old dredging-boxes, worn-out brushes, gallipots, vials, things that it is impossible the most necessitous person can ever want, but which the women, who preside on these occasions, will not leave behind if it was to save your soul. They'd keep the cart ten minutes to stow in dirty pipes and broken matches, to show their economy. Then you can find nothing you want for many days after you get into your new lodgings. You must comb your hair with your fingers, wash your hands without soap, and go about in dirty gaiters... Our place of final destination – I don't mean the grave, but No. 4 Inner Temple Lane – looks out upon a gloomy churchyard-like court, called Hare Court, with three trees and a pump in it. Do you know it? I was born near it, and used to drink at that pump when I was a Rechabite of six years old... On Wednesdays is my levee. We play at whist, eat cold meat and hot potatoes, and any gentleman that chooses smokes... Here I hope to set up my rest, and not quit till Mr. Powell, the undertaker, gives me notice that I may have possession of my last lodging. He lets lodgings for single gentlemen."

On the 7th of June, a few days after moving in, Charles wrote to Coleridge that his new chambers were "far more commodious and roomy [than those at Mitre Court Buildings had been]. I have two rooms on the third floor and five rooms above, with an inner staircase to myself, and all new painted, etc., and all for £30 a year! I came into them on Saturday week; and on Monday following Mary was taken ill with the fatigue of moving; and affected, I believe, by the novelty of the home she could not sleep, and I am left alone with a maid quite a stranger to me, and she has a month or two's sad distraction to go through. What sad large pieces it cuts out of life! – out of her life, who is getting rather old; and we may not have many years to live together. I am weaker, and bear it worse than I ever did. But I hope we shall be comfortable by and by. The rooms are delicious, and the best look backwards into Hare Court… trees come in at the window, so that it is like living in a garden".

However, he was still in the process of adjusting to his new home. "I try to persuade myself it is much pleasanter than Mitre Court; but alas the household gods are slow to come in a new mansion. They are in their infancy to me; I do not feel them yet. How I hate and dread new places!"

Once Mary had recovered from her latest bout of illness and was settled back at her new home, she discovered an adjoining garret of four unoccupied rooms, seemingly without an owner. Over the course of time, Charles and Mary stealthily and gradually appropriated them to their own use. In the event, as nobody ever came forward to claim them, they were at liberty to utilise this welcome extra space throughout their whole tenure of No. 4 Inner Temple Lane. The rooms proved to be of inestimable value to Charles who, as Martin explained, was able to write in them "in secrecy and silence as much alone as if he were in a lodging in the midst of Salisbury Plain".

Once Charles and Mary had properly settled into their new home, the weekly gatherings which had originally been established at Mitre Court Buildings really came into their own. Previously held on Wednesdays, these levees (to use Charles's own term for them) now became an established feature of Thursday evenings. Several of the regular attenders have left valuable accounts of these occasions.

Charles's friend, Thomas Talfourd, who was a judge, a Member of Parliament and a literary critic, sets the scene for us. "Now turn to No. 4 Inner Temple Lane, at ten o'clock, when the sedater part of the company are assembled, and the happier stragglers are dropping in from the play. Let it be any autumn or winter month, when the fire is blazing steadily… The furniture is old-fashioned and worn; the ceiling low, and not wholly unstained by traces of the 'great plant', though now virtuously forborne; [Charles clearly having made another attempt to give up smoking at this time]; but the Hogarths, in narrow black frames, abounding in infinite thought, humour and pathos, enrich the walls; and all things wear an air of comfort and hearty English welcome. Lamb himself, yet unrelaxed by the glass, is sitting with a sort of Quaker primness at the whist-table, the gentleness of his melancholy smile half lost in his intentness on the game; his partner, Godwin, (the majestic expression of his large head not disturbed by disproportion of his comparatively diminutive stature), is regarding his hand with a philosophic but not a careless eye; Captain Burney, not only venerable because so young in spirit, sits between them; and Henry Crabb Robinson, who alone now and then breaks the proper silence, to welcome some incoming guest, is his happy partner – true winner in the game of life, whose leisure achieved early, is devoted to his friends."

Captain Burney was the brother of the novelist Fanny Burney, author of *Evelina* (1778). Among the company on some occasions might also be the Captain's son, Martin, about whom little is known, except that he was devoted to Charles and Mary and eventually became a barrister on the western circuit. Sometimes, the "broad, burly, jovial bulk" of Charles's brother, John, might be seated at another whist table, hero "of the slender clerks of the old South-Sea House, whom he sometimes introduces to the rooms of his younger brother, surprised to learn from them that he is growing famous". The absent-minded and eccentric poet, George Dyer, was often in attendance, and Hazlitt may well "slouch in" after a visit to the theatre, "where his stubborn anger... has been softened by Miss Stephens's angelic notes, which might 'chase anger, and grief, and fear, and sorrow, and pain from mortal or immortal minds'... Meanwhile, Becky lays the cloth on the sidetable, under the direction of the most quiet, sensible and kind of women – who soon compels the younger and more hungry of the guests to partake largely of the cold roast lamb or boiled beef, the heaps of smoking roasted potatoes, and the vast jug of porter, often replenished from the foaming pots which the best tap of Fleet Street supplies. Perfect freedom prevails... [and] as the hot water and its accompaniments appear, and the severities of whist relax, the light of conversation thickens: Hazlitt, catching the influence of the spirit from which he has lately begun to abstain, utters some fine criticism with struggling emphasis; Lamb stammers out puns suggestive of wisdom... the various driblets of talk combine into a stream, while Miss Lamb moves gently about to see that each modest stranger is duly served; turning now and then, an anxious loving eye on Charles, which is softened into a half-humorous expression of resignation to inevitable fate, as he mixes his second tumbler! This is on ordinary nights... but there is a difference on great extra nights, gladdened by 'the bright visitations' of Wordsworth or Coleridge: – the cordiality is the same, but a sedater wisdom prevails... When Coleridge came, argument, wit, humour, criticism were hushed; the pertest, smartest, and the cleverest felt that all were assembled to listen; and if a card-table had been filled, or a dispute begun before he was excited to continuous speech, his gentle voice, undulating in music, soon 'Suspended whist, and took with ravishment/The thronging audience'."

Inevitably, Charles was at the very heart of these gatherings. Without him, after all, they would not have happened. He was, declared Hazlitt, "the most delightful, most provoking, the most witty and sensible of men. He always made the best pun, and the best remark in the course of the evening. His serious conversation, like his serious writing, is his best. No one ever stammered out such fine, piquant, deep, eloquent things in half a dozen sentences as he does. His jests scald like tears: and he probes a question with a play upon words. What a keen, laughing, hare-brained vein of home-truth felt! What choice venom. How often did we cut into the haunch of letters, while we discussed the haunch of mutton on the table! How we skimmed the cream of criticism! How we got into the heart of controversy! How we picked out the marrow of authors! 'And in our flowing cups, many a good name and true was freshly remembered.' They were but the old everlasting set – Milton and Shakespeare, Pope and Dryden, Steele and Addison, Swift and Gay, Fielding, Smollett, Sterne, Richardson, Hogarth's prints, Claude's landscapes, the cartoons at Hampton Court, and all those things that, having once been, must ever be. The Scotch Novels had not then been heard of: so we said nothing about them… I cannot say that the party at Lamb's were all of one description. There were honorary members, lay-brothers. Wit and good-fellowship was the motto inscribed over the door. When a stranger came in, it was not asked, 'Has he written anything?' – We were above that pedantry; but we waited to see what he could do. If he could take a hand at piquet, he was welcome to sit down. If a person liked anything, if he took snuff heartily, it was sufficient… But we abhorred insipidity, affectation and fine gentlemen".

The friendship between Charles and Hazlitt did not always run smoothly as the years passed. As was the case with Coleridge, theirs was an attraction of opposites; their personalities were chalk and cheese. "Each man was ripe for the other, and for a while their intimacy was close and cordial," Lucas explained. "But although Lamb never wavered in his admiration of Hazlitt's intellectual gifts – though he thought him in his saner moments 'one of the finest spirits breathing' – Hazlitt made it very difficult for the flame of friendship to burn with any steady radiance. Indeed he made no friends in the ultimate sense of the word. He valued too much his independence, the right to say what he thought. [However,] Hazlitt felt towards Lamb a sentiment of personal kindness and esteem that was not extended, even in kind, to any other individual."

Like Charles, Hazlitt was a confirmed Londoner at heart (by adoption if not by birth: he was a native of Maidstone in Kent), and he loved to feel the paving stones beneath his feet. In spite of that, however, after meeting Sarah Stoddart in 1806 through Charles and Mary, he moved with her to the village of Winterslow in Wiltshire where, after their marriage, they moved into Middleton Cottage in 1808. Stanley Jones, writing in his *Life of Hazlitt* (1989), describes Sarah as "one who was perhaps clumsily, even at times crudely unconventional, but who was also cheerful, practical, (except in a foreseeing sense), and possessed of a little money, with the prospect of more to come". Perhaps slightly ominously, she could be "a very pleasant companion, fun-loving and high-spirited, but in addition eccentric, erratic, and strong-willed, with little of the demure refinement expected of the well brought up young ladies of those days".

Middleton Cottage had been left to Sarah in a bequest, and Charles and Mary were easily persuaded to pay them a couple of visits there. They planned originally to travel into Wiltshire sometime during July 1809, but the journey had to be postponed because Mary suffered another period of mental illness. This episode coincided with the publication of the two-volume *Poetry for Children*, advertised as "entirely original, by the Author of *Mrs. Leicester's School*" although, in fact, Charles also contributed a small number of poems to the collection. The book was soon allowed to drift out of print, but some of the poems were subsequently anthologised. "The verses... have much charm and sweetness," wrote Lucas, "and they form another illustration of the imaginative power of this old bachelor and old maid (to use Lamb's phrase) in divining what things interest children, and of the tenacity of their memory of their own infancy. Throughout the two little volumes charity, tolerance, thoughtfulness – those watchwords of the two authors – are much insisted upon, directly and indirectly."

On the 30th of October, Charles was able to inform Coleridge that "I have just come off a journey from Wiltshire, where I have been with Mary on a visit to Hazlitt. The journey has been of infinite service to her. We have had nothing but sunshiny days and daily walks from eight to twenty miles a day; have seen Wilton, Salisbury, Stonehenge &c. [Mary's] illness lasted but six weeks; it left her weak, but the country has made us whole". Jones wrote that "the boisterous Lamb, determined to make the most of his annual holiday, may 'for the joke's sake' have dragged the unwilling Hazlitt (who, however, was an indulgent host before he was a frowning republican) to the celebration of King George's golden jubilee on the 23rd of October in Salisbury, with the bands, the parades, the bonfires, the fireworks, and the bottled stout; but it is more likely that they stayed to cast a mild eye on the lesser festivities at Winterslow".

Later, on the 7th of November, Mary wrote to Sarah Hazlitt: "The dear, quiet, lazy delicious month we spent with you is remembered by me with such regret, that I feel quite discontent and Winterslowsick. I assure you, I never passed such a pleasant time in the country in my life, both in the house and out of it, the card playing quarrels, and a few gaspings for breath after your swift footsteps up the high hills excepted; and those drawbacks are not unpleasant in the recollection. We have got some salt butter to make our toast seem like yours, and we have tried to eat meat suppers, but that would not do, for we have left our appetites behind us...".

Towards the end of his life Hazlitt recalled, in his *Farewell to Essay Writing* (completed in February 1828) how, during the Lambs' two visits (Charles and Mary travelled to Winterslow again in 1810), he "used to walk out at this time with Mr. and Miss Lamb of an evening, to look at the Claude Lorraine skies over our heads melting from azure into purple and gold, and to gather mushrooms, that sprung up at our feet, to throw them into our hashed mutton at supper". Unlike their visit of the previous year, Charles and Mary's second holiday with the Hazlitts, which took place during July, was not one of unvarnished happiness. There was much distress at nearby Salisbury, for example, where the bank had failed. "The city is full of weeping and wailing," Charles wrote to his friend Basil Montagu. "Everybody in the town kept money at it, or has got some of its notes. Some have lost all they had in the world. It is the next thing to seeing a city with the plague within its walls. The Wilton people are all undone; all the manufacturers there kept cash at the Salisbury bank; and I do suppose it to be the unhappiest county in England this, where I am making holiday."

Following their return home, Charles told Hazlitt, "Our pleasant excursion has ended sadly for one of us. You will guess I mean my sister. She got home very well (I was very ill on the journey) and continued so till Monday night, when her complaint came on, and she is now absent from home." Mary's attack lasted well into September. Charles observed somewhat ruefully that "travelling is not good for us".

Charles produced a few rhyming stories for children at this time, and they were subsequently published by Godwin, but his more important work during this period appeared in Leigh Hunt's short-lived political and literary quarterly magazine, *Reflector*. It ceased publication after only four numbers, owing to lack of funds and despite rising sales figures, but not before Charles had contributed some of his 'liveliest effusions', according to the editor. These included *Bachelor's Complaint on the Behaviour of Married People*, which later became an Elia essay; and the critical essays, *On the Tragedies of Shakespeare* and *On the Genius and Character of Hogarth*.

***

In 1812, Charles became a landed proprietor, when he inherited from his godfather, Francis Fielde, a seventeenth-century thatched cottage quaintly named Button Snap, situated in the hamlet of Cherry Green, near the village of Westmill, a few miles north of Puckeridge in Hertfordshire. It was the first – and only – property that he ever owned, and it gave him initially a certain degree of pride. In his Elia essay, *My First Play* (1821), Charles explained that by his godfather's "…testamentary beneficence, I came into the possession of the only landed property which I could ever call my own… When I journeyed down to take possession, and planted foot on my own ground, the stately habits of the donor descended upon me, and I strode (shall I confess the vanity?) with larger paces over my allotment of three-quarters of an acre, with its commodious mansion in the midst, with the feeling of an English freeholder that all betwixt sky and centre was my own".

Button Snap consisted of four rooms, a barn, and the quantity of land mentioned by Charles in his description of the property. The origin of its highly unusual name is somewhat obscure, although Reginald Hine, in *Charles Lamb and his Hertfordshire* (1949), suggests that it could perhaps be a corruption of 'Buryton's Knapp', "so styled from the rising ground or knob or knap on which the cottage stands, close to the traces of an ancient moat surrounding the old Bury (or manor) of the

DeJany family of Westmill Green". When Hine was examining the title deeds to Button Snap at the Hertfordshire Records Office one day, "a small printed card fell out of the bundle on to the floor", he explained. "It was the trade card of the 'Crown' at Penrith, with due commendation of its 'new post-chaise, its Mail Coach, and its Coffee Room'. It is an unusual document of title; but then Lamb was an unusual character. On the way to visit Coleridge… in Keswick, he may have been well-received – good provender, nappy ale, honest usage and fair reckoning – and may have preserved the card in the hope of revisiting the inn."

In the event, Charles never lived at Button Snap; the cottage was occupied by a tenant, Mr. Sargus, at the time he inherited it. In February 1815, he gave Sargus notice to quit, as he had decided to part with the property. "The rent that was due at Michaelmas," he wrote, "I do not wish you to pay me. I forgive it you, as you may have been at some expenses in repairs." Button Snap was sold for the sum of £50. (Francis Fielde had acquired the freehold of the cottage in 1779 for £20.) "Life in a country cottage," reflected Hine, "no, it was not to be, and… we must admit that in our mind's eye, we cannot see this restless man, with the fever of London in his very blood, dwindling down into a country cottager. Always he desired to be where he was not; in London he longed for Hertfordshire; in Hertfordshire he longed for London. [This was] written by Lamb when he was, with the pendulum swing of his heart, aching to be back in London": "Let no native Londoner imagine that health and rest, innocent occupation, interchange of converse, sweet and recreative study, can make the country anything better than odious and detestable."

Yet, Button Snap may have proved to be just the ideal spot where "with 'creation's beautiful workmanship' about him [Charles] might have produced his masterpiece", Hine continued, "or have let the hours drift by 'in idleness day long', strolling out in the soft afternoons to Spice Croft, Common Nuttings, Lapping Ley, Washing Wells, Knights Hill, or Tillers End; and at night sitting and nodding over his piquet and porter and pipes. If he needed intellectual stimulus, he could have found it listening to young Thomas Babington Macaulay, who was then (1814–15) being tutored at Aspenden Hall which stood… what Lamb would call 'about one mischievous boy's stone-throw' away… Here he might have given up the unwholesome habit of drinking strong spirits o' nights, and might have betaken himself to 'lamb's-wool', the name then applied to an innocent and invigorating beverage consisting of roasted apples, sugar and ale".

Furthermore, Charles always claimed that he found it so difficult to write in London on account of his friends constantly calling in upon him and disturbing the flow of his concentration. Remote Button Snap would certainly have solved that problem! "Here, with fewer to aid and abet him in the keeping of late hours, and learning at last to burn the candle at neither end, he would have gone to his bed less 'winy and smoky', and have held it no fallacy 'that we should lie down with the lamb'." Hine believed "here perhaps he might have sat in his own cottage parlour, not in the parlour of the Westmill 'Woolpack', and by the grace of God could have written his long promised but unaccountably hitherto delayed *Confessions of a Water Drinker*… Often it has been wondered why Lamb should have disposed of his godfather's gift within the indecent space of three years. If any man lived for his friends, it was Charles Lamb, some of whom lived on him. Most of the impecunious ones lived precariously in London… The explanation I would offer is that Godwin, or more likely Hazlitt, was once again needing money. It is significant that, when the indenture of feoffment conveying the cottage into 'the more prudent hands' of Thomas

Greg of Broad Street Buildings, London, was executed on 15th February 1815, the signature of Charles Lamb... was witnessed by William Hazlitt".

Nevertheless, until the day that Charles drew his final breath, "London's streets, streets, streets, markets, theatres, churches... lamps lit at night, pastry-cooks' and silver-smiths' shops... noise of coaches, drowsy cry of mechanic watchman at night, the bucks reeling home drunk, inns of court with their learned air, old bookstalls", all these things were his life's blood.

As for the later history of Button Snap, it was owned for many years following the Second World War by the Charles Lamb Society. It acquired the property in 1949 and subsequently leased it to tenants. However, the cottage was sold in 1985, reputedly because of the rising maintenance costs, and is now in private hands. (Button Snap is *not* open to the public.)

To remind us of Charles's connection with the cottage, a bas-relief medallion depicting his head and shoulders reclines at a slightly jaunty angle on a grass verge adjacent to his former property. It could previously be found hanging on a wall at the offices of the Westminster Bank Limited in Southampton Buildings, Holborn (where Charles once had lodgings). A bronze tablet placed beside the medallion explains that it was presented to the Charles Lamb Society by the Westminster Bank on the company's removal from its premises on the 4th of February 1965.

By 1814, in deference to Mary's always uncertain health, and in recognition of the strain that the weekly gatherings placed on her fragile condition, the frequency of the Lambs' levees was reduced to once a month. Then, the following year, early and welcome intimations of his retirement came to Charles, when his duties were lightened and his salary doubled at the East India House. Charles yearned to be freed from the yoke with a passion, and longed for the day when he could leave Leadenhall

Street behind him once and for all. Then, at last, he would be free to spend his time writing, reading and wandering at will.

In the meantime, he made the best use of such leisure as came his way. For example, during the late spring of 1815, he paid a return visit to Mackery End, accompanied by Mary (whom he refers to as his devoted 'cousin Bridget', in the nostalgic Elia essay he wrote about the old farmhouse in 1821). Together with Charles's friend, Barron Field, the trio boarded a coach travelling northwards from London to Luton, where they proposed to visit the house of the Earl of Bute, intending to view a painting by Raphael which was on public view there. However, on their arrival they discovered that the house was closed but, deciding not to waste their journey, "we walked two miles through the most beautiful park I ever saw by the side of a river", Mary wrote to a friend in May. "When we left the park we followed its course five or six miles till it conducted us to a farmhouse where a great-aunt of mine once dwelt and where I spent some portion of every year in my younger days; the last visit I made there I had the care and sole management of my little brother Charles, then an urchin of three or four years, he then under my sole guidance."

Charles was more reluctant than Mary to enter the grounds of the old farmhouse that had once been such a welcome playground for them both, but Mary was resolute. "Three or four dogs barking at me enough to frighten me from any other farmhouse in England did not deter me from going in by myself," she declared. However, once he was persuaded by his sister to 'overcome his scruples' and join with her in the adventure, Charles's joy in coming upon his former childhood retreat is evident.

"The sight of the old farmhouse; though every trace of it was effaced from my recollection, affected me with a pleasure which I had not experienced for many a year. For though I had forgotten it, we had never forgotten being there together, and we had been talking about Mackery End all our lives, till memory on my part became mocked with a phantom of itself, and I thought I knew the aspect of a place, which, when present, O how unlike it was to that which I had conjured up so many times instead of it!

"Still the air breathed balmily about it... Bridget's was a more waking bliss than mine, for she easily remembered her old acquaintance again – some altered features, of course, a little grudged at. At first, indeed, she was ready to disbelieve for joy; but the scene soon reconfirmed itself in her affections – and she traversed every outpost of the old mansion, to the woodhouse, the orchard, the place where the pigeon-house had stood, (house and birds were alike flown) – with a breathless impatience of recognition which was more pardonable perhaps than decorous at the age of fifty-odd. But Bridget in some things is behind her years.

"The only thing left was to get into the house – and that was a difficulty which to me singly would have been insurmountable; for I am terribly shy in making myself known to strangers and out-of-date kinsfolk. Love, stronger than scruple, winged my cousin in without me; but she soon returned with a creature that might have sat to a sculptor for the image of Welcome. It was the youngest of the Gladmans, who, by marriage with a Bruton, had become mistress of the old mansion... She was born too late to have remembered me. She just recollected in early life to have had her cousin Bridget once pointed out to her, climbing a stile. But the name of kindred, and of cousinship, was enough... In five minutes we were as thoroughly acquainted as if we had been born and bred up together; we were familiar, even to the calling each other by our Christian names... We were made welcome by husband and wife equally – we and our friend that was with us… The fatted calf was made ready, or rather was already so, as if in anticipation of our coming; and after an appropriate glass of native wine, never let me forget with what honest pride this hospitable cousin made us proceed to Wheathampstead, to introduce us (as some new-found rarity) to her mother and sister Gladmans, who did indeed know something more of us… When I forget all this, then may my country cousins forget me; and Bridget no more remember that in the days of weakling infancy I was her tender charge – as I have been her care in foolish manhood since – in those pretty pastoral walks, long ago, about Mackery End in Hertfordshire."

Charles held the spot and its wider environs in nostalgic remembrance all his life. As the First World War poet, Edward Thomas, observed, Charles "was a good Londoner, but a good Hertfordshire man too, a lover of pure, gentle country, – cornland, copse and water – and of gardens refined out of it. What he saw he put down almost exactly, a little enriched, perhaps, certainly a great deal touched by the pathetic that comes of looking backward, and never more so than when he wrote of the country, because he had never known it except as a place deliberately resorted to for rest and change of air, since he was a child at Blakesware… and at Mackery End."

On a practical level, as Hine pointed out, Charles knew the country "acre by acre, mile by mile, alehouse by alehouse, parish by parish. Whenever he could escape from the 'dry drudgery of the desk's dead wood' he would head off in the direction of Hertfordshire, slowly journeying to those places he loved best on earth".

***

A letter from Mary to Wordsworth's sister-in-law, Sara Hutchinson, dated the 20th of August 1815, relates details of another excursion. "Last Saturday was the grand feast day of the India House Clerks. I think you must have heard Charles talk of his yearly turtle feast," she wrote. "He has been lately much wearied with work, and glad to get rid of all connected with it he used Saturday, the feast day being a holiday, borrowed the Monday following, and we set off on the outside of the Cambridge Coach from Fetter Lane at eight o'clock and we were driven into Cambridge in great triumph by Hell Fire Dick five minutes before three... Journeys used to be tedious torments to me, but seated out in the open air I enjoyed every mile of the way – the first twenty miles was particularly pleasing to me, having been accustomed to go so far on that road in the Ware Stage Coach to visit my Grandmother in the days of other times.

"In my life, I never spent so many pleasant hours together as I did at Cambridge. We were walking the whole time – out of one college into another. If you ask me which I like best I must make the children's traditionary unoffending reply to all enquirers – 'BOTH!' I liked them all best. The little gloomy ones, because they were little gloomy ones. I felt as if I could live and die in them and never wish to speak again. And the fine grand Trinity College. Oh how fine it was! And King's College Chapel, what a place! I heard the Cathedral service there, and having been no great church goer of late years, THAT and the painted windows and the general effect of the whole thing affected me wonderfully.

"I certainly like St. John's College best. I had seen least of it, having only been over it once, so, on the morning we returned, I got up at six o'clock and wandered into it by myself – by myself indeed, for there was nothing alive to be seen but one cat, who followed me about like a dog...

"On the Sunday we met with a pleasant thing. We had been congratulating each other that we had come alone to enjoy, as the miser his feast, all our sights greedily to ourselves, but having seen all we began to grow flat and wish for this and t'other body with us, when we were accosted by a young gownsman whose face we knew, but where or how we had seen him we could not tell, and were obliged to ask his name... He turned out a very pleasant fellow – shewed [sic] us the insides of places – we took him to our Inn to dinner, and drank tea with him in such a delicious college room, and then again he supped with us. We made our meals as short as possible, to lose no time, and walked our young conductor almost off his legs. Even when the fried eels were ready for supper and coming up, having a message from a man who we had bribed for the purpose that we might see [a portrait of Cromwell at Sidney-Sussex College], who was not at home when we called to see him, we sallied out again and made him a visit by candlelight – and so ended our sights. When we were setting out in the morning our new friend came to wish us goodbye, and rode with us as far as Trumpington. I never saw a creature so happy as he was the whole time he was with us; he said we had put him in such good spirits that [he] should certainly pass an examination well that he is to go through in six weeks in order to qualify himself to obtain a fellowship. Returning home down old Fetter Lane I could hardly keep from crying to think it was all over." Charles added a note of his own at the end of the letter. "Mary was in silent raptures all the while there, and came home riding thro' the air triumphing as if she had been graduated."

Significantly, perhaps, Mary's illness returned during the month following their visit to Cambridge, reinforcing Charles's poignant conclusion that travelling was not good for them. However, if he genuinely believed that to be the case, he must have been a glutton for punishment, as the 23rd of September 1816 finds him writing thus to Wordsworth: "Mercy on me, what a traveller I have been since I wrote to you last! What foreign wonders have been explored! I have seen Bath, King Bladud's ancient well, fair Bristol, seed-plot of suicidal Chatterton, Marlbro', Chippenham, Calne, famous for nothing in particular that I know of – but such a vertigo of locomotion has not seized us for years. We spent a month at the last named Borough – August – and such a change has the change wrought in us that we could not stomach wholesome Temple air, but are absolutely rusticating (O the gentility of it) at Dalston, about one mischievous boy's stone's throw off Kingsland Turnpike, one mile from Shoreditch church – thence we emanate in various directions to Hackney, Clapton, Totnam[sic], and such like romantic country. That my lungs should ever prove so dainty as to fancy they perceive differences of air! But so it is, tho' I am almost ashamed of it… I am purging off the foul air of my once darling tobacco in this Eden [and] snuffling up pure gales…".

Writing to Sara Hutchinson in November, Mary also reflects on their 'Dalston rustication', during the course of which Charles would have made his way to and from the East India House in Leadenhall Street each working day. "Reckoning our happy month at Calne, we have had quite a rural summer," wrote Mary, "and have obtained a very clear idea of the great benefit of quiet – of early hours and time intirely [sic] at one's own disposal, and no small advantages these things are; but the return to old friends, the sight of old familiar faces round me, has almost reconciled me to occasional headaches and fits of peevish weariness – even London streets, which I sometimes used to think it hard to be eternally doomed to walk through before I could see a green field, seem quite delightful."

This rural interlude had been prompted by Charles's desire to give up smoking. Mary believed that if she could prise her brother away from his familiar haunts, and from the people in whose company he habitually smoked, then there was at least a slender chance of success. Their lodgings were "quite countrified", Mary told Sara Hutchinson. "I thought if we stayed but a week it would be a little rest and respite from our troubles, and we made a ten weeks' stay, and very comfortable we were, so much so that if ever Charles is superannuated on a small pension, which is the great object of his ambition, and we felt our income straitened, I do think I could live in the country entirely; at least I thought so while I was there, but since I have been at home I wish to live and die in the Temple where I was born. We left the trees so green it looked like early autumn and can see but one leaf, 'the last of its clan' on our poor old Hare Court trees. What a rainy summer! – and yet I have been so much out of town and have made so much use of every fine day that I can hardly help thinking it has been a fine summer. We calculated we walked three hundred and fifty miles while we were in our country lodging. One thing I must tell you, Charles came round every morning to a shop near the Temple to get shaved."

Furthermore, Mary was pleased to report that "Charles smoked but one pipe while we were at Dalston, and he has not transgressed much since his return. I hope he will only smoke now with his fellow-smokers, which will give him five or six clear days in the week". Dalston suited Charles and Mary well, and they retreated to furnished lodgings there for brief periods on several occasions over the years, whenever one or both of them felt the need to escape from the social demands of their London life or to recover their health.

***

After living for much of their lives at various sets of chambers in the Temple, the time came in October 1817 when Charles and Mary moved from their much-loved native place, never to settle there again. In a joint letter to Dorothy Wordsworth, dated the

Bas relief medallion of Charles Lamb, on the roadside verge outside Button Snap.

21st of November, they relate – each in their own inimitable style – the circumstances of this latest upheaval. Charles struck an uncharacteristically melodramatic note in his account. "Here we are transplanted from our native soil," he declared. "I thought we never could have been torn up from the Temple. Indeed, it was an ugly wrench, but like a tooth, now 'tis out, and I am easy. We never can strike root so deep in any other ground."

Mary's tone was one of acceptance and inevitability. "We have left the Temple. I think you will be sorry to hear this… Our rooms were dirty and out of repair, and the inconveniences of living in chambers became every year more irksome, and so, at last, we mustered up resolution enough to leave the good old place, that so long had sheltered us, and here we are, living at a brazier's shop, No. 20, in Russell Street, Covent Garden, a place all alive with noise and bustle; Drury Lane Theatre in sight from our front, and Covent Garden from our back windows. The hubbub of the carriages returning from the play does not annoy me in the least," she went on, "strange that it does not, for it is quite tremendous. I quite enjoy looking out of the window, and listen to the calling up of the carriages, and the squabbles of the coachmen and link boys. It is the oddest scene to look down upon; I am sure you would be amused with it. It is well I am in a cheerful place, or I should have many misgivings about leaving the Temple."

When Charles moved from the Temple, it marked for him the end of one era and the dawn of another. The door to his past was firmly closing but, in fact, had he known it, he was on the threshold of a new life. He was soon to embark on the work that would make him renowned; securing his permanent place in the history of English literature.

Chapter Seven

A Brief Romantic Interlude

Charles's final removal from the Temple was followed the next year, during the summer of 1818, by what was a true milestone in his literary life: the publication of *The Works of Charles Lamb* (in two volumes). He was understandably slightly irritated that the doyen of publishers, John Murray, had refused the proposal, but the firm of Olliers was swift to issue the work. He was clearly pleased with the result, as this lighthearted letter to Charles and James Ollier, dated the 18th of June, suggests: "Dear Sir (whichever opens it)... I find my books, whatever faculty of selling they may have (I wish they had more for your/my sake) are admirably adapted for giving away. You have been bounteous."

By now, Charles was forty-three years old and eagerly looking forward to what he believed would be his still-distant retirement from the East India House. No doubt he had convinced himself, also, that the best – and the bulk – of his literary work was behind him; hence the reason for assembling this collected edition of the articles, essays, literary and theatrical criticism and verse that he most wished to preserve in a more permanent form. Much of his work would originally have appeared in various periodicals and magazines over the years which, by their very nature, come and go as their star either rises or falls. A writer's work can easily be lost to

Framed portrait of Charles Lamb, with signatures of founder members of the Charles Lamb Society.

future generations as a result. His dramatic poem, *John Woodvil*, his prose drama, *Mr. H.*, together with his novel, *Rosamund Gray* were also included, as was *The Old Familiar Faces* which, over two centuries later, still remains his best-known and most-loved poem.

The dedication was to Coleridge. "You will smile to see the slender labours of your friend designated by the title of *Works*," he wrote, "but such was the wish of the gentlemen who have kindly undertaken the trouble of collecting them, and from their judgement could be no appeal. It would be a kind of disloyalty to offer to anyone but yourself a volume containing the early pieces, which were first published among your poems, and were fairly derivatives from you and them. Some of the Sonnets, which shall be carelessly turned over by the general reader, may happily awaken in you remembrances, which I should be sorry should be ever totally extinct – the memory of summer days and of delightful years – even so far back as to those old suppers at our old… Inn, when life was fresh, and topics exhaustless, – and you first kindled in me, if not the power, yet the love of poetry, and beauty, and kindliness. The world has given you many a shrewd nip and gird since that time, but either my eyes are grown dimmer, or my old friend is the same, who stood before me three and twenty years ago – his hair a little confessing the hand of time, but still shrouding the same capacious brain, – his heart not altered…".

On the whole, the two volumes of Charles's *Works* were generously received by the critics on their publication. Charles himself seems to have taken their appearance in his stride; but in writing as in his life generally he was not a person to shower himself with compliments. "I am pleased with your friendly remembrances of my little things," he wrote to Southey on the 26th of October. "I do not know whether I have done a silly thing or a wise one, but it is of no great consequence. I run no risk, and care for no censures. My bread and cheese is stable as the foundations of Leadenhall Street, and if it hold out as long as the 'foundations of our Empire in the East', I shall do pretty well. You and [William Wordsworth] should have had your presentation copies more ceremoniously sent, but I had no copies when I was leaving town for my holidays, and rather than delay, commissioned my bookseller to send them thus nakedly."

Lucas had no doubt Charles "really believed that these volumes did contain his final representative [work], for although we know him to have looked forward to leisure and ease, there is no reason to suppose that he expected any renaissance of literary power or activity; and yet [with the notable exception of *The Old Familiar Faces*] it is not by anything in his *Works* that he is popularly known at all today, but by writings that were not even thought of until two years later".

***

A slender and rare thread of romantic interest entered Charles's life during the year following the publication of his *Works*. During the summer of 1819, the popular and highly successful singer and actress Fanny Kelly was in London and appearing at the Lyceum (off the Strand) in a variety of roles. Born Frances Maria in 1790, in Brighton, she came from a theatrical family. Her father was a minor character actor but, more significantly from Fanny's point of view, her uncle was Michael Kelly, a well-known tenor of the day, who became one of the most sought-after singers on the London stage. In addition, he was an established actor, composer and musical director. An interesting first-hand impression of him is given in *The Autobiography of Leigh Hunt*. "He had a quick, snappish, but not ill-natured voice, and a flushed, handsome, and good-humoured face, with the hair about his ears. The look was a little rakish or so, but very agreeable… Actor, indeed, he was none, except inasmuch as he was an acting singer, and not destitute of a certain spirit in everything he did. Neither had he any particular power as a singer, or even a voice… The little snappish tones I spoke of were very manifest on the stage: he had short arms, as if to match them, and a hasty step and yet, notwithstanding these drawbacks, he was heard with pleasure, for he had taste and feeling. He was a delicate composer... and he selected so happily from other composers, as to give rise to his friend [Richard Brinsley] Sheridan's banter, that he was an 'importer of music and composer of wines' (for he once took to being a wine merchant)."

Fanny studied music with her famous uncle, and it was in his production of *The Dramatick Romance of Blue Beard* (for which he also composed the score) that she made her professional stage debut – as one of the chorus of peasants – at the precociously young age of seven in January 1798. This took place at the Drury Lane Theatre, where Fanny would subsequently appear in leading roles on many occasions over the years to come.

There is a tantalising glimpse of Fanny at this very young stage of her life in Charles's Elia essay, *Barbara S—* (1825). In the guise of an elderly actress, Mrs. Crawford, looking back over her theatrical life, to the early days of her career when playing some child's part she was overpaid one week, he is actually recalling the occasion when Fanny, still only a little girl at the time, was erroneously given double wages on pay day by the treasurer of Drury Lane. Fanny had related this incident to Charles herself. Whether or not she struggled with the temptation to return the overpayment as old Mrs. Crawford confessed she had done in the essay, is not entirely clear, but the inference is that Fanny did the right thing, although not without a certain amount of soul-searching. "A strength not her own was revealed to [*Barbara S—*] – a reason above reasoning – and without her own agency, as it seemed (for she never felt her feet to move), she found herself transported back to the desk she had just quitted, and her hand in the old hand of [the treasurer], who in silence took back the refunded treasure... From that moment a deep peace fell upon her heart, and she knew the quality of honesty... I have heard her say that it was a surprise, not much short of mortification to her, to see the coolness with which the old man pocketed the difference, which had caused her such mortal throes."

In January 1819, when Fanny had left London to embark upon a three-month tour prior to starting her engagement at the Lyceum, she found on her arrival at Bath (the first stop on her itinerary) that Charles, writing under the by-line of 'A London Correspondent', had contributed an extremely flattering article about her acting abilities to the *Bristol Journal*. "This lady has long ranked among the most considerable of our London performers," he enthused. "If there are one or two of greater name, I must impute it to the circumstance that she has never burst upon the town at once in the full maturity of her powers; which is a great advantage to debutantes who have passed their probationary years in Provincial Theatres. We do not hear them tuning their instruments. But she has been winning her patient way from the humblest gradations to the eminence which she has now attained on the self-same boards which supported her first in the slender pretensions of a chorus-singer...".

Charles, who had been a lover of the theatre since his early childhood, and who was now contributing reviews of theatrical productions to Leigh Hunt's *Examiner*, attended several of Fanny's London performances and had fallen completely under her spell. She was already acquainted with Charles and Mary to some degree, having been an occasional guest at their gatherings at 4 Inner Temple Lane and Great Russell Street.

According to her biographer, Basil Francis, in *Fanny Kelly of Drury Lane* (1950), "The habit grew of 'dropping in on the Lambs' on the way home from the theatre, either escorted or alone, and Fanny quickly became accepted, first as an 'honorary member, lay-sister' and then as a 'full member'... At first she must have been a little in awe of the great ones whom she met, and would listen with respectful attention to the gems which fell from the lips of as magnificent a group of conversationalists as it would be possible to imagine: Coleridge, Hazlitt, Wordsworth perhaps, Leigh Hunt... Soon she took her rightful part in the conversation and, although she was no blue stocking, her natural intelligence assured her a good hearing.

"She was at her best, of course, on the occasions when the rather overpowering presence of Coleridge was removed (who else COULD talk when Coleridge held the floor!) and the party was brightened by others of her profession... The pleasant intimacy between Fanny and the Lambs grew quickly and she was soon a great favourite with Charles and Mary. Charles was never a good dissembler and he made no secret of the great pleasure he took in her company: a fact that was duly noted by some of his more astute friends."

His laudatory sonnet *To Miss Kelly* was included in his *Works* in 1818:

> *You are not, Kelly, of the common strain,*
> *That stoop their pride and female honour down*
> *To please that many-headed beast the town,*
> *And vend their lavish smiles and tricks for gain;*
> *By fortune thrown amid the actor's train,*
> *You keep your native dignity of thought,*
> *The plaudits that attend you come unsought,*
> *As tributes due unto your natural vein.*
> *Your tears have passion in them, and a grace*
> *Of genuine freshness, which our hearts avow;*
> *Your smiles are winds whose ways we cannot trace,*
> *That vanish and return we know not how -*
> *And please the better from a pensive face,*
> *And thoughtful eye, and a reflecting brow.*

Writing now in the full storm of his infatuation, Charles sent Fanny an injudicious letter on the 20th of July 1819, in which he – again – fulsomely extolled her virtues and even went on to propose marriage. "We had the pleasure, pain I might better call it, of seeing you last night in the new Play. It was a most consummate piece of Acting, but what a task for you to undergo… It has given rise to a train of thinking which I cannot suppress.

"Would to God you were released from this way of life; that you could bring your mind to consent to take your lot with us, and throw off for ever the whole burden of your Profession. I neither expect or wish you to take notice of this which I am writing, in your present over occupied and hurried state – but to think of it at your leisure. I have quite income enough, if that were all, to justify for me making such a proposal, with what I may call even a handsome provision for my survivor. What you possess of your own would naturally be appropriated to those, for whose sakes chiefly you have made so many hard sacrifices. I am not so foolish as not to know that I am a most unworthy match for such a one as you, but you have for years been a principal object in my mind. In many a sweet assumed character I have learned to love you, but simply as F.M. Kelly I love you better than them all. Can you quit these shadows of existence, & come & be a reality to us? Can you leave off harassing yourself to please a thankless multitude, who know nothing of you, & begin at last to live to yourself & your friends?

"As plainly and as frankly as I have seen you give or refuse assent in some feigned scene, so frankly do me the justice to answer me. It is impossible that I should feel injured or aggrieved by your telling me at once, that the proposal does not suit you. It is impossible that I should ever think of molesting you with idle importunity and persecution after your mind [is] once firmly spoken – but happier, far happier, could I have leave to hope a time might come, when our friends might be your friends; our interests yours; our book-knowledge, if in that inconsiderable particular we have any little advantage, might impart something to you, which you would every day have it in your power ten thousand fold to repay by the added cheerfulness and joy which you could not fail to bring as a dowry into whatever family should have the honour and happiness of receiving YOU, the most welcome accession that could be made to it."

Charles was forty-four at this time and Fanny was fifteen years younger. She let him down very gently but nevertheless very firmly in her reply to his proposal, which was delivered by hand to him later the same day.

"An early & deeply rooted attachment has fixed my heart on one from whom no worldly prospect can well induce me to withdraw it [this is believed to have been untrue], but while I thus frankly & decidedly decline your proposal, believe me, I am not insensible to the high honour which the preference of such a mind as yours confers upon me – let me, however, hope that all thought upon this subject will end with this letter, and that you will henceforth encourage no other sentiment towards me than esteem in my private character and a continuance of that approbation of my humble talents which you have already expressed so much and so often to my advantage and gratification."

Charles took Fanny at her word and replied immediately. "Your injunctions shall be obeyed to a tittle. I feel myself in a lackadaisical nohow-ish kind of humour. I believe it is the rain, or something. I had thought to have written seriously, but I fancy I succeed best in epistles of mere fun; puns and that nonsense. You will be good friends with us, will you not? Let what has past [sic] 'break no bones' between us. You will not refuse us them next time we send for them?"

And there the matter rested, at the end of what must have been for both of them a momentous and wearying day. Lucas, however, mentions a "little epilogue", citing a theatre review that Charles wrote for the *Examiner* just under a fortnight later on the 1st of August. The play, at the Lyceum, was called *The Hypocrite*, and it starred Fanny Kelly. "She is in truth not framed to tease or torment even in jest, but to utter a hearty YES or NO; to yield or refuse assent with a noble sincerity. We have not the pleasure of being acquainted with her, but we have been told that she carries the same cordial manners into private life." Lucas described it as "...the prettiest dramatic criticism in the world".

Less than a fortnight after Charles issued his proposal, Fanny wrote to her sister Lydia, who was also an actress, explaining to her what she could not bring herself to write or say in person to Charles. "I was indeed sorry to refuse him, for he shows the most tender and loyal affections. But even at the peril of my decision causing him great despondency, which I rather feared, I could have no other course than to say the truth that I could not accept his offer. I could not give my assent to a proposal which would bring me into that atmosphere of sad mental uncertainty which surrounds his domestic life. Marriage might well bring us both added causes for misery and regrets in later years."

No doubt Fanny also wished to continue working as an actress – she thrived on the theatrical life – and this would have been highly problematic for them both had she decided to accept Charles's proposal. In reality, she would have been obliged to forsake her hard-won successful career. As Francis wrote in his biography of her, "The proposal must have distressed Fanny considerably, for her nature was generous and kindly and she must have shrunk from the obligation that was forced on her, of wounding a very dear friend. She had to refuse him, of course… She respected him, admired him tremendously, as much for his great humanity as for his intellectual attainments – but respect and admiration were not enough. She had already dedicated her life to her career, not in a self-seeking, ambitious manner, but in a wholehearted concern for the theatre as a vital force in the land – she had literally no time for marriage."

However, her refusal of Charles would by no means prove to be the end of Fanny's connection with the Lambs. She continued to attend many of Charles and Mary's social gatherings over the years to come. Crabb Robinson, for example, recalled in a diary entry of the 21st of November 1820, how he "went late to the Lambs' and stayed an hour there very pleasantly. The Wordsworths were there… Politics were hardly touched on, for Miss Kelly stepped in, who drew our attention to a far more agreeable subject. She pleased me much. She is neither young nor handsome, but very agreeable; her voice and manner those of a person who knows her own worth but is at the same time not desirous to assume upon it. She talks like a sensible woman". If nothing else, this diary entry clearly demonstrates that Charles and Fanny had put his ill-judged proposal of the previous year behind them and had been able to resume their former easy relationship. Fanny and Mary also developed a warm friendship of their own over the course of time, with the latter teaching the actress Latin. During the course of a very long life (she died in 1882 aged ninety-two), Fanny inevitably experienced many professional vicissitudes, but one of her more notable and unusual theatrical achievements was to establish a drama school, initially at the Strand theatre, in 1833. This was an important innovation in its day.

***

Barry Cornwall's memoir of Charles gives a vivid impression of him in middle-age, describing him as he appeared to the outside world around the time that his two-volume *Works* was published and also at the time of his proposal to Fanny. "Persons who had been in the habit of traversing Covent Garden," he wrote, "might by extending their walk a few yards into Russell Street have noticed a small, spare man, clothed in black, who went out every morning and returned every afternoon, as regularly as the hands of the clock moved towards certain hours. You could not mistake him. He was somewhat stiff in his manner, and almost clerical in dress; which indicated much wear."

Charles's deeply conservative sartorial style had, in fact, been cultivated from an early age, and it could never be said to have varied throughout his life. He was only twenty-three when he wrote this letter of feigned indignation to Southey: "My tailor has brought me home a new coat, lapelled, with a velvet collar. He assures me everybody wears velvet collars now. Some are born fashionable, some achieve fashion, and others, like your humble servant, have fashion thrust upon them. The rogue has been making inroads, hitherto by modest degrees, foisting upon me an additional button, recommending gaiters, but to come upon me thus, in the full tide of luxury, neither becomes him as a tailor nor the ninth of a man."

Cornwall described Charles's face in middle-age as long and melancholy, "with keen penetrating eyes; and he walked with a short resolute step, City-wards. He looked no one in the face for more than a moment, yet contrived to see everything as he went on. No one who has ever studied the human features could pass by without recollecting his countenance; it was full of sensibility, and it came upon you like a new thought, which you could not help dwelling upon afterwards; it gave rise to meditation and did you good. This small half-clerical man was – Charles Lamb".

Chapter Eight

Inter Elia

The Elia essays, which were destined to immortalise Charles in the pantheon of English literature, started to appear in the *London Magazine* in August 1820. Cornwall believed that "he was almost teased" into writing them but, as Johnson explained in *Lamb Always Elia*, "this was by no means because of excessive vanity… or because of loss of interest in writing. He probably recalled with no great amount of satisfaction his previous efforts to meet the time requirements of periodical publication and their effect upon his own and Mary's naturally nervous temperaments… It was the common human dislike of being bound by any form of task that made Lamb wary of accepting the 'London' assignments. Yet task work he, like most men, be they geniuses or otherwise, needed in order to make him accomplish anything… However it may have happened… his inherent dramatic sense found satisfaction in writing under another name than his own, and it was very much the fashion for magazine writers to take a pseudonym. As Elia, our essayist could be very personal without embarrassment, and could analyse his own nature with a certain imaginative detachment".

Charles once explained his creative predicament to Godwin. "You, by long habits of composition and a greater command over your own powers, cannot conceive of the desultory and uncertain way in which I (an author by fits) sometimes cannot put the thoughts of a common letter into sane prose. Any work which I take upon myself as an engagement will act upon me to torment e.g. when I have undertaken, as three or four times I have, a schoolboy copy of verses for Merchant Taylors' boys, at a guinea a copy, I have fretted over them in perfect inability to do them, and have made my sister wretched with my wretchedness for a week together. The same, till by habit I have acquired a mechanical command, I have felt in making [i.e. writing] paragraphs. As to reviewing, in particular, my head is so whimsical a head, that I cannot, after reading another man's book, let it have been never so pleasing, give any account of it in any methodical way. I cannot follow his train."

The imperceptible merging of reality and fantasy is the defining characteristic of the Elia essays, and Charles readily acknowledged it to be the case from the outset. In a letter to Field, dated the 16th of August 1820, he writes of his first such effort, *The South-Sea House*, "You shall soon have a tissue of truth and fiction impossible to be extricated, the interleavings shall be so delicate, the partitions perfectly invisible."

The novelist and poet, John Cowper Powys, in his book *Visions and Revisions* (1915), averred that "Lamb deliberately cultivates the art of 'transforming the commonplace' …Elia's style is the only thing in English prose that can be called absolutely perfect… [He] cannot say anything, not the simplest thing, without giving it a turn, a twist, a lift, a lightness, a grace, that would redeem the very grease-spots on a scullion's apron. There is no style in the world like it… Every single one of the essays… can be read over and over again, and their cadences caressed as if they were living people's features. And they are living… He has more academic people in his train than anyone has ever had except Shakespeare".

Colebrooke Cottage, Islington

The Quaker poet, Bernard Barton, even went to the trouble of penning a sonnet (which was printed in the *London Magazine* of February 1823), in his attempt to capture the essence of Elia, and to explain the effect the writer had upon him:

Charles Lamb: Man and Brother First

Delightful Author! – unto whom I owe
Moments and moods of fancy and of feeling
Afresh to grateful Memory now appealing,
Fain would I "bless thee – ere I let thee go"!
From month to month has the exhaustless flow
Of thy original mind, its wealth revealing,
With quaintest humour, and deep pathos healing
The world's rude wounds, revived Life's early glow:
And mix'd with this, at times, to earnest thought
Glimpses of truth, most simple and sublime,
By thy imagination have been brought
Over my spirit. From the olden time
Of Authorship thy Patent should be dated,
And thou, with Marvell, Browne and Burton, mated.

Lucas, writing in 1905, believed that "English Literature has nothing that in its way is better than Elia's best. The blend of sanity, sweet reasonableness, tender fancy, high imagination, sympathetic understanding of human nature, and humour, now wistful, now frolicsome, with literary skill of unsurpassed delicacy, makes Elia unique...

"It is by Elia that Lamb stands where he does; and our prose literature probably contains no work more steeped in personality. What Shakespeare's essays would have been like we cannot conjecture; what Lamb's plays were like we know; and the two men technically are not comparable. But in tolerance... in enjoyment of fun, in love of sweetness... in whimsical humour, Lamb and Shakespeare have much in common. Lamb's criticisms of Shakespeare... seem to come from one peculiarly qualified to speak by reason of superior intimacy or familiarity. He writes more as Shakespeare's friend than any other."

Charles reserved the last word on his alter ego to himself, writing in the deeply satirical *Preface by a Friend of the Late*

Elia (1823). "My late friend was in many respects a singular character. Those who did not like him, hated him; and some, who once liked him, afterwards became his bitterest haters. The truth is, he gave himself too little concern what he uttered, and in whose presence. He observed neither time nor place, and would e'en out with what came uppermost. With the severe religionist he would pass for a free-thinker; while the other faction set him down for a bigot... Few understood him; and I am not certain that at all times he quite understood himself. He too much affected that dangerous figure – irony. He sowed doubtful speeches, and reaped plain unequivocal hatred. – He would interrupt the gravest discussion with some light jest; and yet, perhaps, not quite irrelevant in ears that could understand it. Your long and much talkers hated him. The informal habit of his mind, joined to an inveterate impediment of speech, forbade him to be an orator; and he seemed determined that no one else should play that part when he was present. He was petit and ordinary in his person and appearance. I have seen him sometimes in what is called good company, but where he has been a stranger, sit silent and be suspected for an odd fellow; till some unlucky occasion provoking it, he would stutter out some senseless pun (not altogether senseless, perhaps, if rightly taken), which has stamped his character for the evening.

"He has been accused of trying to be witty, when in truth he was but struggling to give his poor thoughts articulation... He was temperate in his meals and diversions, but always kept on this side of abstemiousness. Only in the use of Indian Weed he might be thought a little excessive. He took it, he would say, as a solvent of speech... As the friendly vapour ascended, how his prattle would curl up sometimes with it! The ligaments which tongue-tied him were loosened... He had a general aversion from being treated like a grave or respectable character, and kept a wary eye upon the advances of age that should so entitle him.

He herded always, while it was possible, with people younger than himself. He did not conform to the march of time but was dragged along in the procession. His manners lagged behind his years... The impressions of infancy had burnt into him, and he refused the impertinence of manhood. These were weaknesses; but such as they were, they are a key to explicate some of his writings."

Charles wrote more than fifty Elia essays. It would be invidious to select one title in favour of another, but among those to which the present author most frequently returns are *The South-Sea House*, *The Old Benchers of the Inner Temple*, *A Dissertation on Roast Pig*, *In Praise of Chimney-Sweepers*, *Christ's Hospital Five-and-Thirty Years Ago* and, possibly above all others, *Dream Children: A Reverie*.

***

Against the backdrop of his increasing renown as the author of the Elia essays, Charles made the startling decision to take a holiday abroad; the first and only time he ever did so. By no stretch of the imagination could he and Mary be described as inveterate travellers, and so it is all the more surprising to find them – in June 1822 – embarking on a trip to France, sailing from Brighton to Dieppe. Crabb Robinson wrote in his diary on the 17th: "To call on the Lambs and take leave, they setting out for France next morning. I gave Miss Lamb a letter for Miss Williams, to whom I sent a copy of Mrs. Leicester's School. The Lambs have a Frenchman as their companion, and Miss Lamb's nurse in case she should be ill. Lamb was in high spirits; his sister rather nervous. Her courage in going is great."

Charles had long harboured a desire to see Paris, although he made scant reference in his subsequent writings to what he did and saw during the time he spent in the city. However, he did send an enthusiastic – albeit brief – account of the French capital to the wife of his friend Barron Field. "I and sister are just returned from Paris!...", he wrote on the 22nd of September. "Paris is a glorious picturesque old city. London looks mean and new to it... But they have no St. Paul's or Westminster Abbey. The Seine, so much despised by Cockneys, is exactly the size to run through a magnificent street; palaces a mile long on one side, lofty Edinbro' stone houses on the other. The Thames disunites London and Southwark."

The great-nephew of Mary's nurse later set down his great-aunt's recollections of this holiday. "In Paris Lamb led his own independent life – disappearing sometimes all day, having lived mostly on the river quays on the Odeon side of the Seine, rummaging the bookstalls and print-shops for old books and old prints, returning late at night to the hotel, and skating up the waxed stairs to bed, thoroughly satisfied with his day's work."

On the last day of August, Charles wrote to the Northamptonshire-born poet, John Clare, author of *The Shepherd's Calendar* (1827), that "since I saw you I have been in France, and have eaten frogs. The nicest little rabbity things you ever tasted. Do look about for them. Make Mrs. Clare pick off the hind quarters, boil them plain, with parsley and butter. The fore-quarters are not so good. She may let them hop off by themselves".

Mary was taken ill at Amiens but, fortunately on this occasion, she recovered quickly and was able to enjoy at least some time in Paris, although Charles was obliged to travel back to London ahead of her and return to work. Mary's stay in Paris was enlivened by the fortuitous arrival in the city of Crabb Robinson, who became her escort on various highly enjoyable excursions. Charles had left behind a helpful note for his sister, suggesting to her some places that she might like to explore in the city in his absence. He mentioned some pictures in the

Louvre that she might like to see, "then you must walk all along the Borough side of the Seine facing the Tuileries. There is a mile and a half of print shops and book stalls. If the latter were but English", he could not resist adding. "Then there is a place where the Paris people put all their dead people, and bring 'em flowers and dolls and gingerbread nuts and sonnets and such trifles. And that is all I think worth seeing as sights, except that the streets and shops of Paris are themselves the best sight."

***

In 1823, despite his claim that he always regarded moving house as a hideous experience, Charles decided to change his abode yet again, swapping Russell Street and Covent Garden for pleasantly rural Islington a few miles to the north. "I have a cottage in Colebrooke Row," he wrote to Barton, in a letter dated the 2nd of September. "A cottage, for it is detached; a white house with six good rooms; the New River (rather elderly by this time) runs (if a moderate walking pace may be so termed) close to the foot of the house; and behind is a spacious garden with vines (I assure you), pears, strawberries, parsnips, leeks, carrots, cabbages [etc.]… You enter without a passage into a cheerful dining-room, all studded over and rough with old books; and above is a lightsome drawing-room, three windows full of choice prints. I feel like a great lord…".

Nowadays, Colebrooke Cottage (as it is called and which still stands but is privately owned and *not* open to the public), forms part of one of Islington's most elegant and fashionable Georgian streets. In Charles's day, this thoroughfare would have been thinly populated indeed, with only a scattering of riverside dwellings in the immediate vicinity. The New River, which once flowed in front of Charles's house, is no longer to be seen, having long been filled in and built upon.

The poet and journalist, Thomas Hood, writing about Charles in *Hood's Own*, a miscellany of witty and humorous pieces, described Colebrooke Cottage as "a cottage of Ungentility; for it had neither double coach-house nor wings. Like its tenant, it stood alone… There was a bit of a garden, in which, being as he professed, more fond of 'Men Sects than of Insects', he made probably his first and last observation in Entomology. He had been watching a spider in a gooseberry bush, entrapping a fly. 'Good God' he said, 'I never saw such a thing. Directly he was caught in her fatal spinning, she darted down upon him, and in a minute turned him out, completely [wrapped] in a shroud!'"

As a near neighbour of Charles and Mary (Hood lived for about twenty years in Lower Street, later renamed Essex Road, until 1827) he was eminently well-placed to visit Colebrooke Cottage. Born in 1799, he suffered from chronic ill-health throughout his relatively short life (he died in 1845), but he still managed to write prolifically and humorously. Despite the considerable age difference between him and Charles, the two men, who had known each other for only a few years at this time, got on famously together. Their first meeting had taken place at the offices of the *London Magazine*, when Hood was working as an assistant to the editor. "I was sitting one morning beside our Editor, busily correcting proofs," Hood recalled, "when a visitor was announced, whose name, grumbled by a low ventriloquial voice… calling from the hold through the hatchway, did not resound distinctly on my tympanum. However, the door opened, and in came a stranger, – a figure remarkable at a glance, with a fine head, on a small spare body supported by two almost immaterial legs. He was clothed in sables, of a bygone fashion, but there was something wanting, or something present about him, that certified he was neither a divine, nor a physician, nor a schoolmaster; from a certain neatness and sobriety in his dress, coupled with his sedate bearing, he might have been taken, but that such a costume would be anomalous, for a Quaker in black. He looked still more like (what he really was) a literary Modern Antique, a New-Old Author, a living Anachronism... Meanwhile he advanced with rather peculiar gait, his walk was plantigrade, and with a cheerful 'How d'ye,' and one of the blandest, sweetest smiles that ever brightened a manly countenance, held out two fingers to the editor.

"The two gentlemen in black soon fell into discourse... It was a striking intellectual face, full of wiry lines, physiognomical quips and cranks that gave it great character. There was much earnestness about the brows, and a deal of speculation in the eyes, which were brown and bright... the nose a decided one, though of no established order; and there was a handsome smartness about the mouth. Altogether it was no common face – none of those 'Willow Pattern' ones, which Nature turns out by thousands at her potteries; but more like a chance specimen of the Chinese ware, one to the set – unique, antique, quaint. No one who had once seen it, could pretend not to know it again. In short, his face was original as his figure; his figure as his character; his character as his writings; his writings the most original of the age. After the literary business had been settled, the Editor invited his contributor to dinner, adding 'we shall have a hare and... many friends.' [Lamb] was shy like myself with strangers, so that, despite my yearnings, our first meeting scarcely amounted to an introduction. We were both at dinner, amongst the hare's many friends, but our acquaintance got no farther, in spite of a desperate attempt on my part to attract his notice."

However, it was not long before the two men became firm friends and according to his biographer, Walter Jerrold, Hood was "accorded that most enviable of privileges, the freedom of Colebrooke Cottage". Writing in his *Literary Reminiscences*, Hood gives an account of his first visit there, which took place after Charles had invited him to meet Wordsworth. "With more alacrity than consistent with prudence, stiff joints and a north wind... I put on my great-coat, and in a few minutes found myself for the first time at a door that opened to me as frankly as its master's heart; for without any preliminaries of hall, passage, or parlour, one single step across the threshold brought me into the sitting-room and in sight of the domestic hearth. The room looked brown with 'old bokes', and beside the fire sate [sic] Wordsworth and his sister, the hospitable Elia and the excellent Bridget. As for the Bard of Rydal, his outward man did not, perhaps, disappoint one, but the 'palaver', as the Indians say, fell short of my anticipations. Perhaps my memory is in fault; 'twas many years ago, and, unlike [Boswell] the biographer of Johnson, I have never made Bozziness my business. However, excepting a discussion on the value of promissory notes issued by our younger poets, wherein Wordsworth named Shelley, and Lamb took John Keats for choice, there was nothing of literary interest brought upon the carpet. But, a book man cannot always be bookish. A poet, even a Rydal one, must be glad at times to descend from Saddleback and feel his legs... It is a vulgar error to suppose that an author must be always authoring, even with his feet on the fender. Nevertheless, it is not an uncommon impression, that a writer sonnetises his wife, sings odes to his children, talks essays and epigrams to his friends; and reviews his servants."

Hood went on to reflect that "very pleasant and improving though not of set purpose, to both heart and mind, were those extempore assemblies at Colebrooke Cottage. It was wholesome for the soul but to breathe its atmosphere. It was a House of Call for all denominations. Men of all parties postponed their partisanship, and met as on neutral ground... They left all their hostilities at the door, with their sticks. This forbearance was due to the truly tolerant spirit of the host, which influenced all within its sphere. Lamb, whilst he willingly lent a crutch to halting humility, took delight in tripping up the stilts of pretension. Anybody might trot out his hobby, but he allowed nobody to ride the high horse... he hated anything like cock-of-the-walk-ism and set his face and his wit against [it]. In opposition to the exclusives, he was emphatically an inclusive". Hood's convivial visits to Colebrooke Cottage, "where somebody who WAS somebody, or a literary friend, was sure to drop in", were to continue until, in the autumn of 1827, he and his wife settled in central London.

Another of Charles's Islington neighbours recalled how he "took to the culture of plants... He watched the growth of his tulips with the gusto of a veteran florist and became learned in all their gaudy varieties. He grew enamoured of anemones. He planted, pruned, and grafted; and seldom walked abroad without a bouquet in his button-hole". Birds, too, diverted him. "They congregated upon his grass-plot, perched upon his window-sills, nestled in the eaves of his house-top, responded to his whistle, pecked up his plum-cake... It became one of his amusements to watch their motions."

It is no surprise to find that Charles soon became an habitué of the local hostelries in Islington; smoking his pipe and drinking beer out of a huge tankard, at the Queen's Head in particular. A year later, Leigh Hunt was still lamenting his friend's move away from Covent Garden. "C.L., why didst thou ever quit Russell Street?" he asked. "Why didst thou leave the warm crowd of humanity, which thou lovest so well, to go and shiver on the side of the New River, inticing [sic] thy unwary friends to walk in? Were friends and sitting up at night too attractive? And was there no other way to get rid of them?"

Leigh Hunt is making a slightly mischievous reference here to a potentially tragic – even if comical – incident which occurred outside Colebrooke Cottage in November 1823. It followed a visit by Charles's seriously absent-minded and short-sighted friend, the elderly and eccentric classicist and editor, George Dyer. Twenty years older than Charles and similarly from humble origins (his father was believed to have been a watchman at Wapping), Dyer was also a former Christ's Hospital boy. He became Head of the School before going up to Emmanuel College, Cambridge. Charles related details of the incident in question in a letter to Mrs. Hazlitt shortly after it had occurred. "Yesterday week George Dyer called upon us, at one o'clock (bright noonday)... He sat with Mary about half an hour, and took leave. The maid saw him go out, from her kitchen window, but suddenly losing sight of him, ran up in a fright to Mary. G.D., instead of keeping the slip that leads to the gate, had deliberately, staff in hand, in broad open day, marched into the New River. He had not his spectacles on, and you know his absence. Who helped him out they could hardly tell, but between 'em they got him out, drenched thro' and

Plaque on the wall of Colebrooke Cottage

thro'. A mob collected by that time and accompanied him in. 'Send for the Doctor,' they said, and a one-eyed fellow, dirty and drunk, was fetched from the public house where he lurks, for the sake of picking up water practice; having formerly had a medal from the Humane Society for some rescue. By his advice the patient was put between blankets; and when I came home at 4 to dinner, I found G.D. a-bed, and raving, light-headed, with the brandy and water which the doctor had administered. He sang, laughed, whimpered, screamed, babbled of guardian angels, and would get up and go home; but we kept him there by force; and by next morning he departed sober, and seems to have received no injury. All my friends are open-mouth'd about having paling before the river; but I cannot see, because a lunatic chooses to walk into a river with his eyes open at midday, I am any more likely to be drowned in it, coming home at midnight." Charles declared, in his Elia essay, *Amicus Redivivus* (1823): "I protest, George, you shall not venture out again – no, not by daylight – without a sufficient pair of spectacles – in your musing moods especially. Your absence of mind we have borne, till your presence of body came to be called in question by it… I have nothing but water in my head o'nights since this frightful accident."

Dyer's frequent acts of absent-mindedness were legendary among his circle of friends. Leigh Hunt, for example, recalled the time when Dyer had spent an evening with him at his house on Hampstead Heath. A quarter of an hour after leaving for his chamber at Clifford's Inn, Holborn, Dyer turned up at Hunt's house again. "I think, sir, I have left one of my shoes behind me," he wailed. Which indeed proved to be the case. Seemingly, he had unconsciously removed it during dinner, and did not discover the fact until he had walked quite some distance homewards! Further stories tell of him leaving another friend's house with the coal skuttle instead of his hat; and of emptying ginger or snuff into his teapot instead of tea leaves. Leigh Hunt described him as "an angel of the dusty heaven of bookstalls and the British Museum", adding that his life "was one unbroken dream of learning and goodness".

Chapter Nine

'From Life into Eternity'

Nobody who knew Charles could have been unaware of his longing for retirement. William Wordsworth would certainly have been in no doubt of it. "I grow ominously tired of official confinement," Charles had written to him on the 20th of March 1822. "Thirty years have I served the Philistines, and my neck is not subdued to the yoke. You don't know how wearisome it is to breathe the air of four pent walls without relief, day after day, all the golden hours of the day between ten and four, without ease or interposition… Oh for a few years between the grave and the desk… I dare not whisper to myself a pension on this side of absolute incapacitation and infirmity, till years have sucked me dry… I had thought in a green old age to have retired to Ponder's End (emblematic name, how beautiful!) in the Ware Road, there to have made up my accounts with Heaven and the company, toddling about between it and Cheshunt; anon stretching, on some fine Izaak Walton morning, to Hoddesdon or Amwell, careless as a beggar; but walking, walking, walking ever till I fairly walked myself off my legs, dying walking. [The remark was a prescient one.] The hope is gone. I sit like Philomel all day… with my breast against this thorn of a Desk, with the only hope that some Pulmonary affliction may relieve me. Vide Lord Palmerston's report of the

Clerks in the War Office, by which it appears in 20 years as many clerks have been coughed and catarrhd out of it into their freer graves."

Writing subsequently in his Elia essay, *The Superannuated Man* (1825), he conceded that at least he had Sundays to himself, "but Sundays, admirable as the institution of them is for the purposes of worship, are for that very reason the very worst adapted of days for unbending and recreation. In particular there is a gloom for me attendant upon a City Sunday, a weight in the air. I miss the cheerful cries of London, the music, and the ballad-singers – the buzz and stirring murmur of the streets. Those eternal bells depress me. The closed shops repel me. Prints, pictures, all the glittering and endless succession of knacks and gewgaws, and ostentatiously displayed wares of tradesmen, which make a week-day saunter through the less busy parts of the metropolis so delightful – are shut out. No bookstalls deliciously to idle over – no busy faces to recreate the idle man who contemplates them ever passing by… Nothing to be seen but unhappy countenances – or half-happy at best – of emancipated 'prentices and little trades folk, with here and there a servant-maid that has got leave to go out, who slaving all the week, with the habit has lost almost all the capacity of enjoying a free hour; and livelily expressing the hollowness of a day's pleasuring. The very strollers in the fields on that day look anything but comfortable.

"But besides Sundays I had a day at Easter, and a day at Christmas, with a full week in the summer to go and air myself in my native fields of Hertfordshire. This last was a great indulgence; and the prospect of its recurrence, I believe, alone kept me up though the year, and made my durance tolerable."

At last, on the 29th of March 1825, Charles was granted early retirement from the East India House and, as Lucas phrased it, "received his freedom and returned to Islington a gentleman at large".

Writing again to Wordsworth in a letter dated the 6th of April, he exclaimed: "Here I am then, after thirty-three years' slavery, sitting in my own room at eleven o'clock this finest of all April mornings, a freed man, with £441 a year for the remainder of my life... I came home FOR EVER on Tuesday in last week. The incomprehensibleness of my condition overwhelmed me. It was like passing from life into eternity. Every year to be as long as three, i.e. to have three times as much real time (time that is my own) in it! I wandered about thinking I was happy, but feeling I was not. But that tumultuousness is passing off, and I begin to understand the nature of the gift. Holydays, even the annual month, were always uneasy joys; their conscious fugitiveness; the craving after making the most of them. Now, when all is holyday, there are no holydays. I can sit at home, in rain or shine, without a restless impulse for walkings. I am daily steadying, and shall soon find it as natural to me to be my own master, as it has been irksome to have had a master. Mary wakes every morning with an obscure feeling that some good has happened to us... I eat, drink and sleep as sound as ever. I lay no anxious schemes for going hither and thither, but take things as they occur. Yesterday I excursioned twenty miles; today I write a few letters. Pleasuring was for fugitive play-days; mine are fugitive only in the sense that life is fugitive. Freedom and life co-existent!"

Writing to Barton on the same day, Charles said, "My spirits are so tumultuary with the novelty of my recent emancipation, that I have scarce steadiness of hand, much more mind, to compose a letter. I am free, B.B. – free as air! 'The little bird that wings the sky/knows no such liberty'... I will live another fifty years; or, if I live but ten, they will be thirty, reckoning the quantity of real time in them, i.e. the time that is a man's own."

Nevertheless, there were some signs of an early ambivalence in Charles's attitude towards his retirement, now that this long dreamed-of state had been granted to him. "I would not serve another seven years for seven thousand pounds," he added in his letter to Barton, before striking a rather different note as he related how he "went and sat among 'em all at my thirty-three years' desk yester morning; and deuce take me, if I had not yearnings at leaving all my old pen-and-ink fellows, merry sociable lads, at leaving them in the lurch, fag, fag, fag, fag! – The comparison of my own superior felicity gave me anything but pleasure".

He expanded upon these sentiments in *The Superannuated Man*. "I have been fain to go among them once or twice since, to visit my old desk-fellows – my co-brethren of the quill – that I had left in the state militant. Not all the kindness with which they received me could quite restore to me that pleasant familiarity I had heretofore enjoyed among them. We cracked some of our old jokes, but methought they went off but faintly. My old desk; the peg where I hung my hat were appropriated to another. I know it must be, but I could not take it kindly. Devil take me, if I did not feel some remorse – beast, if I had not, – at quitting my old compeers, the faithful partners of my toil for six-and-thirty years, that smoothed for me with their jokes and conundrums the ruggedness of my professional road. Had it been so rugged then after all, or was I a coward simply? Well, it is too late to repent; and I also know, that these suggestions are a common fallacy of the mind on such occasions. But my heart smote me. I had violently broken the bands betwixt us. It was at least not courteous. I shall be some time before I get quite reconciled to the separation."

Elsewhere in this essay, he returns to the theme explored in his letters to Wordsworth and Barton; of the mixed feelings he experienced in the immediate wake of his retirement. "For the first day or two I felt stunned, overwhelmed," he wrote. "I could only apprehend my felicity; I was too confused to taste it sincerely. I wandered about thinking I was happy, and knowing that I was not. I was in the condition of a prisoner in the old Bastile, suddenly let loose after a forty years' confinement. I could scarce trust myself with myself... It seemed to me that I had more time on my hands than I could ever manage. From a poor man, poor in Time, I was suddenly lifted up into a vast revenue; I could see no end of my vast possessions; I wanted some steward, or judicious bailiff, to manage my estates in Time for me...

"Among the strange fantasies which beset me at the commencement of my freedom, and of which all traces are not yet gone, one was, that a vast tract of time had intervened since I quitted [the East India House]. I could not conceive it as an affair of yesterday. The clerks with whom I had for so many years, and for so many hours in each day of the year, been closely associated, being suddenly removed from them they seemed dead to me... Time stands still in a manner to me. I have lost all distinction of season. I do not know the day of the week, or of the month. Each day used to be individually felt by me in its reference to the foreign post days; in its distance from, or propinquity to, the next Sunday. I had my Wednesday feelings, my Saturdays nights' sensations. The genius of each day was upon me distinctly during the whole of it, affecting my appetite, spirits, etc... [Now] all days are the same."

Martin explained how Charles "was put to all sorts of devices to waste his cherished time! He rehung his Titians, his Da Vincis, his Hogarths, and his other beloved prints. He marshalled his Chelsea china shepherds and shepherdesses in groups and singly all about the rooms He rearranged the ragged veterans of his library... Few of them were lettered on the spine, and his reply to a silly somebody, who asked how he knew them, was: 'How does a shepherd know his sheep?'.

"Out of doors he planted and pruned and grafted; and got into a row with an old lady who owned the next garden. He sat under his own vine and contemplated the growth of nature. He explored his new neighbourhood, hunted up ancient hostelries, and made comparisons of their sundry and divers taps. He prowled about Bartholomew Fair, drinking in delight of its penny puppet-shows, and its other 'celebrated follies', as they had been contumeliously called by John Evelyn, a visitor there nearly two centuries earlier. He took long walks into the country with Tom Hood's erratic dog, the aptly named Dash, who imposed outrageously on Lamb's good nature; and went on excursions with Mary farther afield – notably to Enfield...".

In July 1825, Charles and Mary took lodgings with a Mrs. Leishman at Chase Side, Enfield. Charles had been feeling 'under the weather' for some time, as Crabb Robinson explained to Dorothy Wordsworth, in a letter dated the 6th of June. "Poor Lamb is very unwell. His illness is however I trust a mere attack on his nerves arising out of what he is so little able to bear – troublesome business. The widow of his late brother [John, who had died in 1821] is just dead and he is the sole executor. The will WILL give him trouble. And he was harassed during his illness by the necessity of making frequent journeys."

Indeed, the will was still proving troublesome for Charles nearly four years later, as he explained in a letter to Proctor dated January 1829. "The fact is I am involved in a case which has fretted me to death, and I have no reliance except on you to extricate me. I am sure you will give me your best legal advice... My brother's widow left a will, made during the lifetime of my brother, in which I am named sole executor, by which she bequeaths forty acres of arable property, which it seems she held... unknown to my brother. For God's sake assist me, for the case... deprives me of sleep and appetite."

***

If Charles had hoped to recover his health while at Chase Side, he was sorely disappointed. "I came home in a week from Enfield, worse than I went," he wrote to his friend, Hone, on the 30th of September. "My sufferings have been intense, but are abating. I begin to know what a little sleep is. My sister has sunk under her anxieties about me. She is laid up, deprived of reason for many weeks to come, I fear. She is in the same house, but we do not meet. It makes both worse. I can just hobble down as far as the 'Angel' once a day; further kills me... If you come this way any morning, I can only just shake you by the hand. This gloomy house does not admit of making my friends welcome."

On a cheerier note, Sarah Flower Adams, friend of Coleridge, Leigh Hunt and Southey, and author of the hymn, *Nearer My God to Thee*, has provided a charming account of an evening spent at Colebrooke Cottage at the end of 1825, on which occasion Coleridge happened to be present. "The character of Charles Lamb's person was in total contrast to that of Coleridge. His strongly marked, deeply lined face, furrowed more by feeling than age, like an engraving by Blake, where every line told its separate story, or like a finely chiselled head done by some master in marble, where every touch of the chisel marked some new attribute. Yet withal there was so much sweetness and playfulness lurking about the corners of the mouth, that it gave to the face the extraordinary character of flexible granite. His figure was small even to spareness. It was as if the soul within, in its constant restless activity, had worn the body to its smallest possibility of existence.

"There was an equal amount of difference in his conversation from that of Coleridge, as there was in his person. It was not one uninterrupted flow, but a periodical production of sentences, short, telling, full of wit, philosophy, at times slightly caustic, though that is too strong a word for satire which was of the most good-natured kind. There was another essential point of difference. In Coleridge might be detected a certain consciousness of being listened to, and at times an evident getting up of phrases, a habit almost impossible to be avoided in a practised conversationalist. In Charles Lamb there was a perfect absence of this; all that he said was choice in its humour, true in its philosophy; but the racy freshness, that was like an atmosphere of country air about it, was better than all; the perfect simplicity, absence of all conceit, child-like enjoyment of his own wit, and the sweetness and benevolence that played about the rugged face, gave to it a charm in no way inferior to the poetical enjoyment derived from the more popular conversation of his friend.

"Another difference might be observed; that Coleridge's metaphysics seemed based in the study of his own individual nature more than the nature of others, while Charles Lamb seemed not for a moment to rest on self, but to throw his whole soul into the nature of circumstances and things around him. These differences served only to heighten the enjoyment of witnessing the long-enduring genuine friendship existing between the two – the three (for why should Mary be excluded?)...

"At last it was time for Coleridge to go, for he had the walk to Highgate all before him. There was an affectionate parting, as if they had been boys rather than men, and it seemed to concentrate their lives into that minute. It recalled the meetings and partings of other days; the wanderings by the lakes; the many minglings in social union; a whole host of recollections seemed to crowd around and enclose them in a magic circle. Coleridge lingered on the threshold, as if he were leaving what had been a part of his heart's home for many years; and again he who had been his companion in many a mountain ramble, many a stroll in dale, forest and mead... would fain have kept up the old companionship even though it was night... [but]

another grasp of the hand, and a kiss of affection on Mary's cheek, and Coleridge was gone."

***

On the whole, Charles's retirement proved to be a classic example of the old adage, 'Be careful what you wish for'. "Lamb would have been wiser had he not retired," Lucas believed, "but after taking a long holiday for recuperation, returned to his office work and remained in harness all his life. As from time to time he tells his friends, his leisure became a burden to him, aggravated by his remoteness from London, and also by the circumstance that his sister, who was now getting on to be an elderly woman (she was sixty-one at the time of his retirement) grew increasingly ill with each visitation of her malady, thus leaving him with longer and longer periods of loneliness. No one was less fitted than he to be solitary and unemployed. To be happy and well he needed a little routine, friends after work and a city environment, whereas instead of this he had nothing to do; for weeks and weeks no company but his own thoughts, and his home either in Islington or in distant Enfield Chase. It is no wonder that his health declined and his frailties increased. When his sister was well; when visitors found their way to his door… when the enthusiasm for work was upon him; Lamb was again himself."

Charles severed his connection with the *London Magazine* (the home of his *Elia Essays*) in 1825, after the business had changed hands, and he told Southey that he would write for it no more. His final contribution, the essay *Stage Illusion*, appeared in the August number. However, he agreed to write a series of articles for the editor of the *New Monthly Magazine*, with the umbrella heading of 'Popular Fallacies'. These included such titles as 'That a bully is always a coward'; 'That ill-gotten gains never prosper'; 'That handsome is as handsome does', etc. The first of these slender pieces, of which he wrote well over a dozen, appeared in January 1826. On the 26th of September of that year, however, Charles wrote to Wordsworth that "I have at last broke [sic] the bonds of business... never to put 'em on again. I pitch Colborn [editor of the *New Monthly*] and his magazine to the divil [sic]. I find I can live without the necessity of writing, tho' last year I fretted myself to a fever with the hauntings of being starved. Those vapours are flown. All the difference I find is that I have no pocket money: that is, I must not pry upon an old book stall, and cull its contents as heretofore, but shoulders of mutton, Whitbread's entire, and Booth's best, abound as formerly."

Even so, he seemed quite buoyed up by the prospect of having more literary work to do, as he explained in a letter to Barton of the same day's date. "I am going through a course of reading at the [British] Museum: the Garrick plays… I have two thousand to go thro'; and in a few weeks have despatched the tythe of 'em. It is a sort of office to me; hours ten to four, the same. It does me good. Man must have regular occupation, that has been used to it." The extracts that Charles made and subsequently gathered together were destined to appear in Hone's *Table Book* of 1827.

Sadly, however, these more contented interludes proved to be few and far between. "Too often he was alone, lacking any fixed purpose, sick and dejected. The history of his life between 1825 and 1834," Lucas concluded, "makes sad reading."

***

An antidote to the frequent tedium and solitariness of his days, however, was provided for Charles in the person of Emma Isola. During the summer of 1820, Charles and Mary had spent their holiday at Cambridge where, at some point during their stay, they had encountered Emma for the first time at the house of friends in Trumpington Street. At this time, Emma was eleven years of age. Her mother was dead and she was the daughter of Charles Isola of Cambridge University. Her grandfather, Agostino, was an Italian emigre who had settled in the town. He had become an extremely popular teacher of his native language (he had once numbered William Wordsworth among his pupils), and he was a much-loved figure locally. His son, who was somewhat diffident in his manner, had been elected in 1797 to a junior ceremonial post (with the unlikely title of Esquire Bedell) within the university. It seems that, on this very first meeting with the young girl, Charles and Mary invited Emma to spend Christmas 1820 with them as the following letter, dated the 27th of January 1821 and addressed to her aunt, Miss Humphreys (with whom the young girl lived) suggests. "Dear Madam," Charles began, "Carriages to Cambridge are in such request… that we have found it impossible to procure a conveyance for Emma before Wednesday, on which day between the hours of 3 and 4 in the afternoon you will see your little friend, with her bloom somewhat impaired by late hours and dissipation, but her gait, gesture, and general manners (I flatter myself) considerably improved. My sister joins me in love to all true Trumpingtonians… and begs me to assure you that Emma has been a very good girl, which, with certain limitations, I must myself subscribe to. I wish I could cure her of making dog's ears in books, and pinching them on poor Pompey [Charles and Mary's current dog] who, for one, I dare say will heartily rejoyce [sic] at her departure."

In the event, Emma's visit had been slightly delayed, owing to the fact that Mary became ill again over Christmas, albeit only briefly. However, it did not prevent the young girl from enjoying herself when she belatedly reached Great Russell Street.

"I arrived quite safe and Miss Lamb was at the Inn waiting for me," she reported to her aunt. "The first night I came we went out to spend the evening. The second night Mr. Lamb took me to see the wild beasts at Exeter 'Change. Saturday night being Twelfth Night I went to a party and did not return until four in the morning. Yesterday, Miss Lamb took me to the theatre at Covent Garden. I cannot tell you how much I liked it. I was so delighted."

Emma's father died in 1823 and, following his death, Charles and Mary adopted Emma as their own daughter. Charles always wrote and spoke of her with great affection. As a schoolgirl and, later, as a governess in the household of Mrs. Williams, wife of the rector of Fornham, near Bury St. Edmunds in Suffolk, Emma spent all of her holidays with Charles and Mary, enlivening their home and their existence in the process. Over the years she gradually established herself as an invaluable part of their household, increasingly supplying much-needed practical and emotional support.

***

We first hear of Edward Moxon in a letter (quoted earlier) from Charles to William Wordsworth, dated the 26th of September 1826. At that time, Moxon was nearly twenty-five (he was born in December 1801) and employed as a clerk in the publishing firm of Longman's. "The Bearer of this [letter]," wrote Charles, "is my young friend Moxon, a young lad with a Yorkshire head [he was from Wakefield], and a heart that would do honour to a more southern county; no offence to Westmorland. He is one of Longman's best hands, and can give you the best account of 'The Trade' as 'tis now going, or stopping… Moxon is but a tradesman in the bud yet, and retains his virgin Honesty… He is a friendly serviceable fellow, and thinks nothing of lugging up a cargo of the newest novels once or twice a week... to Colebrooke to gratify my sister's passion for the newest things. He is author besides of a poem which for a first attempt is promising... Moxon has petitioned me by letter (for he had not the confidence to ask it in London) to introduce him to you during his holydays [sic]; pray pat him on the head; ask him a civil question or two about his verses, and favour him with your autograph. He shall not be further troublesome."

Moxon subsequently became a poet of some note in his day, after Charles had succeeded in encouraging him to publish his first collection of verse in 1826. The volume, *The Prospect and Other Poems* garnered some favourable reviews at the time. Given the limited circles in which they moved, it is not surprising that, in the fulness of time, Emma's and Moxon's paths would eventually cross.

Chapter Ten

'...None to Call Me Charley Now'

In late September 1827, Charles and Mary, accompanied by Emma, moved out of Colebrooke Cottage, leaving London ten or so miles to the south. They settled at the decidedly airier and more rural Enfield Chase in Middlesex, not far from their former lodgings with Mrs. Leishman (which they briefly occupied again immediately prior to their move). Two hundred years earlier the spot had been a favourite royal hunting park, stretching for over 8,000 acres to the west of the village of Enfield. Their house, "the prettiest, compactest house I ever saw", declared an enthusiastic Charles, was built in the early nineteenth century, and thus still quite new when the Lambs moved into it. Its age, style and surroundings were all a far cry from Charles's birthplace in the Temple. Thomas Westwood, the thirteen-year-old son of their new next-door neighbour (also Thomas, but later dubbed 'Gaffer' Westwood by Charles) recalled seeing them for the first time shortly after their arrival. Writing in 1866, he explained, "My first glimpse of the Lamb household... is as vivid in my recollection as if it were of yesterday... Leaning idly out of window, I saw a group of three issuing from the gambogey [yellow]-looking cottage close at hand: a slim middle-aged man, in quaint uncontemporary habiliments; a rather shapeless bundle of an old lady in a bonnet like a mob cap and a young girl, while before them bounded a riotous dog [Hood's irrepressible Dash] holding a board with 'This House to Let' in his jaws."

Dash, it need hardly be said, was very much a character in his own right, and for a while at Colebrooke Cottage he was a much-loved and enlivening addition to Charles and Mary's circle whenever he was 'on loan' to them from Hood for one reason or another. P.G. Patmore (father of the poet Coventry Patmore), who had been introduced to Charles by Hazlitt in 1824, described Dash as "a large and very handsome dog, of a very curious breed... The Lambs (albeit spinster and bachelor) were not addicted to 'dumb creatures'; but this dog was an especial pet – probably in virtue of his owner, who was a great favourite with them) – and he always accompanied Lamb on his long rambling daily walks... During these interminable rambles – heretofore pleasant in virtue of their profound loneliness and freedom as respected all companionship and restraint, – Lamb made himself a perfect slave to this dog, whose habits were of the most extravagantly errant nature, for, generally speaking, the creature was half-a-mile off from his companions, either before or behind, scouring the fields or roads in all directions, scampering up or down all manners of streets, and keeping Lamb in a perfect fever of irritation and annoyance; for he was afraid of losing the dog when it was out of sight, and yet could not persuade himself to keep it IN sight by curbing its roving spirit. Dash knew Lamb's weaknesses on these particulars as well as he did himself, and took a due dog-like advantage of it. In the Regent's Park in particular, Dash had his master completely at his mercy; for the moment they got into the ring, he used to get through the paling on to the green sward, and disappear for a quarter of an hour together – knowing perfectly well that Lamb did not dare to move from the spot where he (Dash) had disappeared, till such time as he thought proper to show himself again. And they used to take this particular walk much oftener than they otherwise would, precisely because Dash liked it and Lamb did not.

"I had often admired this dog; but was not a little astonished one day when Lamb and his sister came to dine with us at North End (near Fulham), where we then lived, and brought Dash with them all the way on foot from Islington! The undertaking of the pig-driver... must have been nothing to this of the dear couple, in conducting Dash through London streets. It appeared, however, that they had not brought him out this time for his own [relaxation], but to ask me if I would have him, 'if it were only out of charity,' Miss Lamb said half in joke, half in earnest, 'for if they kept him much longer, he would be the death of Charles!'."

Subsequently, Patmore did agree to take Dash off Charles's hands, "...and I soon found, as I expected, that his wild and wilful ways were a pure imposition upon the easy temper of Lamb, and that as soon as he found himself in the hands of one who knew what dog-decorum was, he subsided into the best bred and best behaved of his species".

On the 18th of September, Charles wrote to Hood informing his friend how the move to Enfield was progressing. "We have got books into our new house and we shall get in by Michael's Mass [sic] [the 29th of September] ...To change habitations is to die to them; and in my time I have died seven deaths. But I don't know whether every change does not bring with it a rejuvenescense. 'Tis an enterprise; and shoves back the sense of death's approximating, which, tho' not terrible to me, is at all times particularly distasteful. My house-deaths have generally been periodical, recurring after seven years; but this last is premature by half that time. Cut off in the flower of Colebrooke! ...Our new domicile is no manor-house; but new, and externally not inviting, but furnish'd within with every convenience:

capital new locks to every door, capital grates in every room; with nothing to pay for incoming; and the rent £10 less than the Islington one... I get it for £35, exclusive of moderate taxes. We think ourselves most lucky.

"It is not our intention to abandon Regent Street and West End perambulations (monastic and terrible thought!), but occasionally to breathe the fresher air of the metropolis."

Despite his heavy preoccupation with the move, Charles did not neglect to take the opportunity of providing a helping hand to his young friend Moxon, as this letter dated the 25th of September and written to the publisher Colborn confirms. "I beg leave in the warmest manner to recommend to your notice Mr. Moxon... if by any chance you should want a steady hand in your business, or know of any Publisher that may want such a one. He is at present in the house of Messrs. Longman & Co., where he has been established for more than six years... A difference respecting salary, which he expected to be a little raised on his last promotion, makes him wish to try to better himself. I believe him to be a young man of the highest integrity and a thorough man of business, and should not have taken the liberty of recommending him, if I had not thought him capable of being highly useful."

Hood was swift to call on Charles once he had settled in at Enfield Chase, although Charles was obliged to discourage the arrival of any visitors at first, as Mary was "taken ill of her old complaint" on the very night before they moved in. When Hood arrived, he found his friend living "in a bald-looking yellowish house, with a bit of a garden, and a wasps' nest convanient [sic] as the Irish say, for one stung my pony as he stood at the door. Lamb laughed at the fun; but, as the clown says, the whirligig of time brought round its revenges. He was one day bantering with my wife on her dread of wasps, when all at once he uttered a horrible shout; a wounded specimen of the species had slyly crawled up the leg of the table, and stung him on the thumb".

Westwood's youthful perspective of the Lambs at the time of their arrival verged, not surprisingly perhaps, upon the satirical in tone, but for a more sympathetic view of Charles and Mary during this period we can turn to the impressions gained of them by a young American artist, Mrs. Mary Balmanno, and gathered during a supper party given by the Hoods at their home in the Adelphi, where they lived between 1827 and 1829. Mrs. Balmanno's account was published in her book, *Pen and Pencil* (1858). "Miss Lamb, although many years older than her brother, by no means looked so, but presented the pleasant appearance of a mild, rather stout, and comely maiden lady of middle age. Dressed with quaker-like simplicity in dove-coloured silk, with a transparent kerchief of snow-white muslin folded across her bosom, she at once prepossessed the beholder in her favour, by an aspect of serenity and peace. Her manners were very quiet and gentle, and her voice low. She smiled frequently, but seldom laughed, partaking of the courtesies and hospitalities of her merry host and hostess with all the cheerfulness and grace of a most mild and kindly nature.

"Her behaviour to her brother was like that of an admiring disciple; her eyes seldom absent from his face. Even when apparently engrossed in conversation with others, she would, by supplying some word for which he was at a loss, even when talking in a distant part of the room, show how closely her mind waited upon his. Mr. Lamb was in high spirits, sauntering about the room, with his hands crossed behind his back, conversing by fits and starts with those most familiarly known to him, but evidently mentally acknowledging Miss Kelly to be the 'rara avis' of his thoughts, by the great attention he paid to every word she uttered. Truly pleasant it must have been to her, even though accustomed to see people listen breathless with admiration while she spoke, to find her words have so much charm for such a man as Charles Lamb.

"He appeared to enjoy himself greatly, much to the gratification of Mrs. Hood, who often interchanged happy glances with Miss Lamb, who nodded approvingly. He spoke much – with emphasis and hurry of words, sorely impeded by the stammering utterance which in him was not unattractive. Miss Kelly (charming, natural Miss Kelly, who has drawn from her audiences more heart-felt tears and smiles than perhaps any other English actress), with quiet good humour listened and laughed at the witty sallies of her host and his gifted friend, seeming as little an actress as it is possible to conceive... Amidst a most amusing mixture of wit and humour, sense and nonsense, we feasted merrily, amidst jocose health-drinking, sentiments, speeches and songs."

***

It was to be many years later, of course, that Westwood set down his boyhood recollections of Charles and Mary at Chase Side. As soon as they had settled in (and Mary had recovered from her latest spell of illness), he enjoyed an immensely privileged position for one so young as himself. "When any notable visitors made their appearance at the cottage," he explained, "Mary Lamb's benevolent tap at my window-pane seldom failed to summon me out, and I was presently ensconced in a quiet corner of their sitting-room, half hid in some great man's shadow. Of the discourse... I have no recollection now; but the faces of some of them I can still partially recall. Hazlitt's, for instance, keen and aggressive, with eyes that flashed out epigram. Tom Hood's, a Methodist parson face: not a ripple breaking through the lines of it, though every word he dropped was a pun, and every pun roused a roar of laughter. Leigh Hunt, with much rabid politics… Miss Kelly's, plain but engaging. (The most… unspoiled of women; the bloom of the child on her cheek, undefaced by the rouge, to speak in a metaphor.) She was one of the most dearly welcome of Lamb's guests. Wordsworth's, farmerish and respectable, but with something of the great poet occasionally breaking out and glorifying forehead and eyes. Then there was Martin Burney, ugliest of men, hugest of eaters, honestest of friends… And George Darley, scholar and poet – slow of speech and gentle of strain: Miss Kelly's constant shadow in her walks amongst the Enfield woodlands." Westwood also recalled that he, too, accompanied Fanny on her walks in the garden and in the fields near the house.

"Miss Kelly, with the heart of a child," he wrote, "had all a child's delight in wild flowers. She had also a passion for little frogs. I was Miss Kelly's frog-catcher. When my scanty honours are counted, let not this one be overlooked. To have been Miss Kelly's frog-catcher… that is something, surely!"

Her biographer, Francis, elaborated the point. "What little it takes to make for happiness! – and what her amazed public would have thought could they have seen the celebrated Miss Kelly stretched full length in a country meadow, with a round-eyed [young lad] at her side, whole-heartedly absorbed in the pretty pastime of scratching the head of a very small frog, to the [young lad's] transparent delight and the frog's manifest enjoyment."

Although Westwood did not conclude his recollections of the Lambs at Enfield until 1872, over forty years after the events he described, his memory of them was still crystal clear. "I see the room now. The brisk fire in the grate, the lighted card-table some paces off, Charles and Mary Lamb and Emma Isola seated round it playing whist; the old books thronging the old shelves; the Titian and Da Vinci engravings on the walls."

Westwood, as he grew older, dabbled a good deal in literature himself. Perhaps he had been influenced by the fact that, in the honourable tradition of old Samuel Salt at the Temple, Charles had given him free rein of his and Mary's library. Although Westwood always considered himself an amateur writer, this did not prevent him from producing a significant piece of work which he compiled with Thomas Satchell. *Bibliotheca Piscatoria, A Catalogue of Books on Angling, The Fisheries and Fish Culture* appeared in 1883, and was described by one reviewer as "a monumental work invaluable to students of the gentle art".

***

Neither Charles nor Mary enjoyed particularly good health after their move to Enfield. Charles's ailments, though largely unspecified, caused him to become very low in spirits, resulting in a loss of motivation to write. At the root of it, no doubt, was the fact that, as she got older, Mary's mental health was gradually becoming more problematic, with the result that Charles spent longer and more frequent periods at home alone. The following letter, written to Barton on the 25th of July 1829, demonstrates that Charles could sometimes descend into deep melancholy. "I have had the loneliest time, near ten weeks, broken by a short apparition of Emma for her holidays, whose departure only deepened the returning solitude, and by ten days I have past [sic] in town. But town, with all my native hankering after it, is not what it was. The streets, the shops, are left, but all old friends have gone." 'Ghost-like, I paced round the haunts of my childhood./ Earth seemed a desert I was bound to traverse,/Seeking to find the old familiar faces', he had written prophetically, as a young man in 1798.

"And in London I was frightfully convinced of this as I passed houses and places, empty caskets now. I have ceased to care, almost about anybody. The bodies I cared for are in graves or dispersed. My old clubs, that lived so long and flourished so steadily, are crumbled away. When I took leave of [Emma] at Charing Cross, 'twas heavy unfeeling rain, and I had nowhere to go. Home have I none and not a sympathising house to turn to in the great city. Never did the waters of heaven pour down on a forlorner head... I got home on Thursday convinced that I was better to get home to my hole at Enfield and hide like a sick cat in my corner. Less than a month I hope will bring home Mary. She is at Fulham, looking better in her health than ever, but sadly rambling, and scarce showing any pleasure in seeing me, or curiosity when I shall come again. But the old feelings will come back again, and we shall drown old sorrows over a game of piquet again. But 'tis a tedious cut out of a life of 64, to lose 12 or 13 weeks every year or two. And to make me more alone, our ill-tempered maid is gone, who with all her airs... was yet a record of better days. The young thing that has succeeded her is good and attentive, but she is nothing. And I have no one here to talk over old matters with. Scolding and quarrelling have something of familiarity, and a community of interest; they imply acquaintance; they are of resentment, which is of the family of dearness.

"I can neither scold nor quarrel at this insignificant implement of household services; she is less than a cat, and just better than a deal dresser. What I can do, and do over-do, is to walk; but deadly long are the days, these Summer all-day days, with but a half-hour's candlelight, and no firelight. I do not write... and can hardly read... I bragged formerly that I could not have too much time. I have a surfeit. With few years to come, the days are wearisome. But weariness is not eternal. Something will shine out to take the load off that flags me, which is at present intolerable."

Charles would have been much cheered, for example, by the visit paid to Enfield Chase by his recently married friend, Charles Cowden Clarke and his wife Mary. Clarke, a

Shakespearian scholar, was born in Enfield, where his father had kept a small school at which John Keats had been a pupil. "During the forenoons and afternoons of this memorable visit," recalled Clarke, "we used to take the most enchanting walks in all directions of the lovely neighbourhood. Over by Winchmore Hill, through Southgate Wood to Southgate and back... Another time, a longer excursion was proposed, when Miss Lamb declined accompanying us, but said she would meet us on our return, as the walk was farther than she thought she could manage. It was to Northaw; through charming lanes, and country by-roads, and we went hoping to see a famous old giant oak-tree there... Mary Lamb was as good as her word – when was she otherwise? And came to join us on our way back and be with us on our reaching home, there to make us comfortable in old-fashioned easy-chairs for 'a good rest' before dinner.

"The evenings were spent in cosy talk, or telling some racy story, or uttering some fine thoughtful remark... His style of playful bluntness when speaking to his intimates was strangely pleasant – nay, welcome: it gave you the impression of his liking you well enough to be rough and unceremonious with you; it showed you that he felt at home with you...

"There is... a point on which we would fain say a word in vindication of noble, high-natured, true-hearted Charles Lamb; a word that ought once and for ever to be taken on trust as coming from those who had the honour of staying under his own roof and seeing him day by day from morning to night in familiar home intercourse – a word that ought once and for ever to set at rest accusations and innuendoes brought by those who know him only by handed down tradition and second-hand report. As so much has of late years been hinted and loosely spoken about Lamb's 'habit of drinking' and of 'taking more than was good for him', we state emphatically – from our own personal knowledge – that Lamb, far from taking much, took very little, but had so weak a stomach that what would have been a mere nothing to an inveterate drinker acted on him like potations 'pottle deep'. We have seen him make a single tumbler of moderately strong spirits-and-water last through a long evening of pipe-smoking and fireside talk; and we have also seen the strange suddenness with which but a glass or two of wine would cause him to speak with more than his usual stammer – nay, with a thickness of utterance and impeded articulation… As to Lamb's own confessions of intemperance, they are to be taken as all his personal pieces of writing… ought to be, with more than a 'grain of salt'."

There were also other happier interludes for Charles, not least when he walked the seventeen or so miles each way from Enfield to Widford, where he would revisit old childhood haunts. The journey was a considerable undertaking, and Charles confessed to sometimes having blisters on his feet afterwards, but he claimed they didn't bother him because he still enjoyed walking so much. On his arrival at Widford, he would visit old friends in the area; in particular, the two sisters, Miss Betsy and Miss Jane, who ran Goddard House School in the village. They were the daughters of the Lamb family's friend from the Temple, Randal Norris, who served as Sub-Treasurer of the Inner Temple. When Norris died early in 1827, Charles wrote wistfully to Crabb Robinson: "In him I have a loss the world cannot make up. He was my friend and my father's friend, for all the life I can remember… Those are the friendships which outlast a second generation. Old as I am waxing, in his eyes I was still the child he first knew me. To the last he called me Charley. I have none to call me Charley now. He was the last link that bound me to the Temple… In him seem to have died the old plainness of manners and singleness of heart. Letters he knew nothing of, nor did his reading extend beyond the Gentleman's Magazine. Yet there was a pride of literature about him from being amongst books (he was librarian), and from some scraps of doubtful Latin which he had picked up in his office of entering students, that gave him very diverting airs of pedantry... His poor good girls will now have to receive their afflicted mother in an unsuccessful hovel in an obscure village in Herts., where they have been long struggling to make a school without effect; and poor deaf Richard [Norris's son], and the more helpless for being so, is thrown on the wide world."

On a far more positive note, however, Lucas reports that "on moving to Widford in 1827, Mrs. Norris quickly took her place as the good angel of her old village [she had been born there]; doctor, nurse, and every one's refuge in trouble. No sooner did the rumour of sickness waft in, than, I gather, Goddard House projected beef tea and jellies into the afflicted home". Happily, Richard continued to live within the family.

A former pupil at Goddard House School, Elizabeth Hunt (later Mrs. Coe), who lived until 1903, remembered Charles from his visits to Widford (where he usually stayed at the mill), and her reminiscences appeared in the *Athenaeum* in June 1902. As such, she provided an invaluable eye-witness account of Charles during his later years. "He always brought a book with him, sometimes several, and he would read or write a great deal. His clothes were rusty and shabby like a poor Dissenting minister's. He was very thin and looked half-starved; partly the effect of high cheek-bones. He wore knee-breeches and gaiters and a high stock. He carried a walking stick with which he used to strike at pebbles. He smoked a black clay pipe. No one would have taken him for what he was, but he was clearly a man apart. He took pleasure in looking eccentric. He was proud of being THE MR. LAMB."

Mrs. Coe went on to recall how Charles would invariably give money to any beggar he encountered in the street, sometimes as much as three shillings! "Poor devil, he wants it more than I do; and I've got plenty," she had heard him remark more than once. She further recalled that, during his visits to Widford, "Mr. Lamb had a favourite seat in a tree in the 'Wilderness' at Blakesware, where he would sit and read for hours... At other times he would watch the trout in the stream, and perhaps feed them, for half the morning. Once or twice he took a rod, but he could never bring himself to fix the worms."

Charles conjured up a vision of the 'Wilderness' in his novel, *Rosamund Gray*. "I have often left my childish sports to ramble in this place," he wrote. "Its gloom and its solitude had a mysterious charm for my young mind, nurturing within me that love of quietness and lonely thinking which has accompanied me to maturer years." It is likely that he now also daydreamed there about the 'fair-hair'd maid' who had lived close by at Blenheims long years ago. For there was a particular reason why Blakesware (the house was demolished in 1822) held a special place in Charles's heart. Visits to the old manor house and the environs of Widford had inspired some of his earliest sonnets. Later, in his Elia essay, *Dream Children: A Reverie* (1822) he refers to 'Alice W...', who was almost certainly Ann Simmons of Blenheims near Blakesware; she was the girl whom he had met when visiting his grandmother and who, had the course of true love proved more obliging, he might possibly have asked to become his wife.

Charles was a youth of seventeen or eighteen when his infatuation with Ann Simmons reached its height, and its sad conclusion. "Charles's battle of Blenheim went against him," declared Hine, "he laid siege to a heart that surrendered to another. But the memory of those seven years remained sweet to him in single unblessedness." Almost thirty years later, writing in his Elia essay, *New Year's Eve* (1821), Charles averred that "I should have pined away seven of my goldenest years, when I was thrall to the fair hair and fairer eyes of Alice W..., than that so passionate a love-adventure should be lost". Being the sensitive soul that he was, Charles no doubt believed that none of his experiences in life – either good or bad – should have been otherwise, for perhaps in the end they all served to shape and nourish the writer that he eventually became. "I would no more alter them than the incidents of some well-contrived novel," he declared. Mary Field, Lucas wrote, is said to have discouraged the intimacy on the grounds that there was insanity in the Lamb family; the truth of which subsequent years were to afford ample proof.

Ann Simmons went on to marry a London pawnbroker and she settled in Leicester Square. A final glimpse finds her a widow, living with her three daughters in Fitzroy Street, a short step from the Tottenham Court Road. Although she was geographically close to Charles for much of their lives, she played no further part in his daily existence. Yet, as Cecil wrote, "for ever after, Ann, with her fair hair and tender blue-eyed glance, was to occupy a special and sanctified place in his recollections: as a middle-aged bachelor he was still to look back wistfully to his unrealised daydream of a happy home with her as his wife and the mother of his children… no one else was to take her place. She remained a unique figure in his life: fragile and unfulfilled as his feeling for her might seem, it was the only thing of its kind in his history, and his relation to her the nearest he ever got to a love affair".

Hine believed, rather fancifully some might say, that "though it was to 'a fair-hair'd maid' at Blenheims that Charles lost his heart, and though the course of true love did never yet run smooth, and though Ann Simmons, spinster of Widford parish, became the spouse of [another], her 'dream children', begotten of the suitor she was forced to reject, were all born in Hertfordshire. You will not find them in any register of baptisms, because dream children are not baptized. You will not find them in any register of burials, because they live for ever".

Chapter Eleven

'Worn to the Poetical Dregs'

In October 1829, spurred on perhaps by a combination of ill-health and low spirits, Charles and Mary took the momentous decision to give up housekeeping for themselves. They had been living together independently in a state of 'double singleness' since their father's death in 1799. They moved in as lodgers with their neighbours, 'Gaffer' Westwood and his wife, as Charles related in a letter to Wordsworth, dated the 22nd of January 1830. "The seasons pass us with indifference. Spring cheers not, nor Winter heightens our gloom. Autumn hath foregone its moralities… Yet as far as last year occurs back… 'twas sufficiently gloomy. Let the sullen nothing pass. Suffice it, that after sad spirits, prolonged through many of its months, as it called them, we have cast our skins, have taken a farewell of the pompous troublesome trifle call'd house-keeping, and are settled down into poor boarders and lodgers at next door, with an old couple, the Baucis and Baucida of dull Enfield. Here we have nothing to do with our victuals but to eat them, with the garden but to see it grow, with the tax-gatherer but to hear him knock, with the maid but to hear her scolded… Butcher, baker, are things unknown to us, save as spectators of the pageant… Yet in the self-condemned obliviousness, in the stagnation, some molesting yearnings of life, not quite kill'd, rise, prompting me

Lamb's Cottage, Church Street, Edmonton

that there was a London, and that I was of that old Jerusalem. In dreams I am in Fleet Market, but I wake and cry to sleep again… What have I gained by health? Intolerable dullness. What by early hours and moderate meals? A total blank. O never let the lying poets be believed, who 'tice men from the cheerful haunts of streets… Confining, room-keeping, thickset winter, is yet more bearable here than the gaudy months. Among one's books at one's fire by candle, one is soothed into an oblivion that one is not in the country.

"Our providers are an honest pair, Dame W— and her husband. He, when the light of prosperity shined on them, a moderately thriving haberdasher within Bow Bells, retired since with something under a competence... hath borne parish offices; sings fine old sea songs at threescore and ten, sighs only now and then when he thinks that he has a son on his hands about fifteen, whom he finds a difficulty in getting out into the world, and then checks a sigh with muttering, as I once heard him prettily, not meaning to be heard, 'I have married my daughter, however'; takes the weather as it comes; outsides it to town in severest season; and o' winter nights tells old stories...

"Under his roof now ought I to take my rest, but that back-looking ambition tells me I might yet be a Londoner! Well, if we ever do move, we have encumbrances the less to impede us; all our furniture has faded under the auctioneer's hammer, going for nothing, like the tarnished frippery of the prodigal, and we have only a spoon or two left to bless us. Clothed we came into Enfield, and naked we must go out of it. I would live in London shirtless, bookless...".

Mary added a postscript to Dorothy Wordsworth at the end of Charles's letter: "I never go to town, nor my brother, but at his quarterly visits at the India House, and when he does, he finds it melancholy, so many of our old friends being dead or dispersed, and the very streets, he says, altering every day... If you knew how happy your letters made us you would write I know more frequently. Pray think of this. How cheerfully should we pay the postage ANY WEEK."

Although London no longer held its former appeal for Charles, one senses that – in his ideal world – he would have swapped rural Enfield for it any day of the week. "Give me old

London at fire and plague times," he wrote to Barton on the 25th of February, "rather than these tepid gales, healthy country air and purposeless exercise… Let me congratulate you on the spring coming in, and do you in return condole with me on the winter going out. When the old one goes seldom comes a better. I dread the prospect of summer, with his all-day-long days. No need of his assistance to make country places dull. With fire and candle-light I can dream myself in Holborn. With lightsome skies shining in to bed-time I can not."

The late winter brought unwelcome and distressing news for Charles and Mary, who were informed at the end of February that Emma lay seriously ill at Fornham, with what was described in the opaque medical terminology of the age as a dangerous 'brain fever'. Whatever the symptoms and severity of her complaint, however, the worst of it was soon over. As early as the 1st of March, Charles was able to write in reply to another letter from Mrs. Williams at Fornham, which had borne sufficiently favourable tidings that "you would forgive me for my nonsense if you knew how light-hearted you have made two poor souls at Enfield, that were gasping for news of their poor friend… We are happier than we hardly know how to bear". Emma was settled at Enfield by the beginning of April. Having travelled to Fornham to collect her, Charles reported their safe arrival home to Mrs. Williams. "I have great pleasure in letting you know that Miss Isola has suffered very little fatigue on her long journey. I am ashamed to say that I came home rather the more tired of the two; but I am a very unpractised traveller. We found my sister very well in health, only a little impatient to see her; and after a few hysterical tears for gladness, all was comfortable again. We arrived here from Epping between five and six. We had in the coach a rather talkative gentleman, but very civil all the way; and took up a servant maid at Stamford. To the latter a participation in the hospitalities of your nice rusks and sandwiches proved agreeable… The former engaged me in a discourse for full twenty miles, on the probable advantages of steam carriages… But when, somewhere about Stanstead, he put an unfortunate question to me as to 'the probability of its turning out a good turnip season' and when I… not knowing a turnip from a potato ground, innocently made answer, 'I believe it depends very much upon boiled legs of mutton,' my unlucky reply set Miss Isola a-laughing to a degree that disturbed her tranquillity for the only moment in our journey. I am afraid my credit sank very low with my other fellow-travellers."

More good news was to follow in the summer of 1830, when Charles's new volume, *Album Verses and Other Poems* became the first book to be issued by Edward Moxon's newly established publishing house; a venture he was able to embark upon after receiving a loan of £500 from Samuel Rogers, a generous literary acquaintance of Charles's. The book was dedicated to Moxon. "It is not for me, nor you," wrote Charles, "to allude in public to the kindness of our honoured Friend, under whose auspices you are become a Bookseller. May that fine-minded Veteran in Verse enjoy life long enough to see his patronage justified. I venture to predict that your habits of industry, and your cheerful spirit, will carry you through the world."

However, Charles was characteristically self-effacing about his latest work itself. "You will see that I am worn to the poetical dregs," he wrote to Barton in June, "condescending to acrostics, which are nine fathom beneath album verses; but they were written at the request of the lady where our Emma is, to whom I paid a visit in April to bring home Emma for a change of air after a severe illness, in which she had been treated like a daughter by the good Parson and his whole family." In August, he thanked Barton for his "warm interest about my little volume; for the critics of which I care the five hundred thousandth part of the tythe of a half-farthing. I am too old a Militant for that. How noble, tho', in Robert Southey to come forward for an old friend... But what a clamour against a poor collection of Album Verses, as if we had put forth an Epic!"

In September came the sad news of Hazlitt's death – after a turbulent life – at his lodgings in Frith Street, Soho. By chance, Charles was lodging temporarily in London at the time, once again at Southampton Buildings, Holborn, and he was one of those old friends who visited Hazlitt during the closing weeks and days of his life. He also attended the funeral which was held at St. Anne's, Soho, when only a few other mourners were present. Perhaps his thoughts tended towards the words that Hazlitt had written about him only five years earlier in *The Spirit of the Age*. "Mr. Lamb has the very soul of an antiquarian. He evades the present; he mocks the future. His affections revert to, and settle on, the past; but then even this must have something personal and local in it to interest him deeply and thoroughly. He pitches his tent in the suburbs of existing manners; brings down the account of character to the few straggling remains of the last generation... No one describes the manners of the last generation so well as Mr. Lamb; with so fine and yet so formal an air; with such vivid obscurity; with such arch piquancy, such picturesque quaintness, such smiling pathos." If those words did float into Charles's mind on that melancholy occasion, hopefully he found some comfort and pleasure in recalling them.

***

Charles had left Enfield for a couple of months, in the hope that a change of scenery would prove beneficial to his – and more particularly to Mary's – health, which had been poor of late. Sadly, their stay in London proved to be of no avail to Mary, as Charles explained sometime later in a doleful letter to Moxon, dated the 12th of November. "I... brought my sister to Enfield being sure that she had no hope of recovery in London. Her state of mind is deplorable beyond any example. I almost fear whether she has strength at her time of life ever to get out of it. Here she must be nursed, and neither see nor hear of anything in the world out of her sick chamber. The mere hearing that Southey had called at our lodgings totally upset her... I dare not write or receive a letter in her presence; every little talk so agitates her. Westwood will receive any letter for me, and give it me privately."

Somehow, despite his travails, Charles managed to find the inner strength to resume some occasional writing including, in 1831, his long comic ballad, *Satan in Search of a Wife*, which was published anonymously by Moxon. It was largely composed during another of Mary's long periods of illness. Subsequent letters that Charles wrote to Moxon suggest that the work did not sell well. "You hinted that there might be something under £10, by and by, accruing to me; 'Devil's Money', ...that I entirely renounce, and abjure all future interest in; I insist upon it... I won't touch a penny of it. That will split your loss one half," he wrote on the 24th of October.

Crabb Robinson, who had lately been abroad for some time, visited Charles and Mary in the middle of October, and recorded his impressions of their life at Enfield during this period. Clearly, he was not greatly impressed by their situation. "I found Lamb and his sister boarding with the Westwoods – good people who, I dare say, take care of them. At least the woman, for W. is an old man and invalid and seems nearly in his dotage. Mrs. W. seems active and kind. Lamb has rendered himself their benefactor by getting a place for their son at Aders' counting-house. They return his services by attentions which he and his sister want, but it is deplorable that he should be reduced to such a state that he has none to associate with but the very lowest of people in attainments. No wonder that he seems very discontented. Both he and Miss L. looked somewhat older... They were heartily glad to see me as it seemed. After dinner, I was anxious to leave them before it was dark...".

On the 2nd of November, Charles was visited by the irascible Scottish historian and philosopher, Thomas Carlyle, the so-called 'Sage of Chelsea' and native of Ecclefechan in Dumfriesshire. He has bequeathed to us in his 'Diary' a startlingly cruel portrait of Charles, which was written following their meeting and with a pen dipped in venom. It is well worth quoting here at some length. "Charles Lamb I sincerely believe to be in some considerable degree insane," he exploded. "A more pitiful, ricketty, gasping, staggering, stammering Tomfool I do not know. He is witty by denying truisms and abjuring good manners. His speech wriggles hither and thither with an incessant painful fluctuation, not an opinion in it, or a fact, or a phrase that you can thank him for – more like a convulsion fit... Besides, he is now a confirmed, shameless, drunkard; asks vehemently for gin and water in strangers' houses, tipples till he is utterly mad, and is only not thrown out of doors because he is too much despised for taking such trouble with him. Poor Lamb! Poor England, when such a despicable abortion is named genius."

Rather aptly in the circumstances, Charles had written ten years earlier in his Elia essay, *Imperfect Sympathies* (1821), "I have been trying all my life to like Scotchmen [sic], and am obliged to desist from the experiment in despair. They cannot like me – and in truth, I never knew one of that nation who attempted to do it... We know one another at first sight. There is an order of imperfect intellects (under which mine must be content to rank) which in its constitution is essentially anti-Caledonian... I was present not long since at a party of North Britons, where a son of Burns was expected, and happened to drop a silly expression (in my South British way) that I wished it were the father instead of the son – when four of them started up at once to inform me that 'that was impossible, because he was dead'. An impracticable wish, it seems, was more than they could conceive... The tediousness of these people is certainly provoking. I wonder if they ever tire one another! In my early life I had a passionate fondness for the poetry of Burns. I have sometimes foolishly hoped to ingratiate myself with his countrymen by expressing it. But I have always found that a true Scot resents your admiration of his compatriot, even more than he would your contempt of him. The latter he imputes to your imperfect acquaintance with many of the words which he uses; and the same objection makes it a presumption in you to suppose that you can admire him!".

Sadly, there was more to come from Carlyle a few decades later and couched in the same vein as his original tirade. On this occasion he described Charles and Mary – somewhat unkindly – as "a very sorry pair of phenomena. Insuperable proclivity to gin, in poor old Lamb. His talk contemptibly small, indicating wondrous ignorance and shallowness, even when it was serious and good-mannered, which it seldom was; usually ill-mannered (to a degree), screwed into frosty artificialities, ghastly make-believe of wit – in fact, more like 'diluted insanity' (as I defined it) than anything of real jocosity, humour or geniality... he was Cockney to the marrow; and Cockneydom, shouting, 'Glorious, marvellous, unparalleled in Nature!' all his days, had quite bewildered his poor head, and churned nearly all the sense out of the poor man... in walking [he] tottered and shuffled; emblem of imbecility bodily and spiritual...".

Fortunately, by the time that Carlyle delivered this second venomous tirade, Charles had been at rest in his coffin for some years. As Lucas justly points out, however, there were far too many people around at the time of Carlyle's first attack who knew Charles at his true worth, and who could personally attest to his humanity and genius, for us to take any account of the 'Sage of Chelsea's' trademark contumely.

If not exactly in defence of Carlyle's rant against Charles, following their meeting in 1831, but perhaps in some mitigation of it, Lucas quotes from an article published in the *British Quarterly Review* of May 1848, in which the author (who may have been personally acquainted with the actual circumstances of that encounter) writes that "Lamb was never partial to the Scotch [sic], and on this evening he was more than usually offensive in his remarks on their character; but when supper appeared, and a bowl of porridge was placed before Carlyle, Lamb's jokes and remarks upon it were so insulting as almost to lead to an open quarrel".

However, a pleasing postscript to this Anglo-Scottish spat occurred during the summer of the following year when the Paisley-born writer, John Wilson, better known by his pseudonym 'Christopher North', of *Blackwood's Edinburgh Magazine* called on Charles at Enfield in July 1832. Moxon was also present on this occasion. They took a long walk and enjoyed a pint together at a local inn; something that would have endeared Wilson to Charles immediately, particularly when he discovered that the celebrated 'Christopher North' shared his own taste for porter. Subsequently, Wilson wrote a charming and conciliatory appraisal of his host. "Charles Lamb ought really not to abuse Scotland in the pleasant way he so often does in the sylvan glades of Enfield; for Scotland loves Charles Lamb; but he is wayward and wilful in his wisdom, and conceits that many a cockney is a better man even than Christopher North. But what will not Christopher forgive to genius and goodness? Even Lamb bleating libels on his native land. Nay, he learns lessons of humanity even from the mild malice of Elia, and breathes a blessing on him and his household in their bower of rest."

The gravestone of Charles and Mary Lamb in All Saints Churchyard, Edmonton

Crabb Robinson went to Enfield to see Charles two weeks after Wilson's visit. "He was in excellent health and in tolerable spirits. He spoke of his sister with composure. She in now in confinement, but he says she suffers nothing. It is only before and after she entirely loses her mind that she is very wretched and suffers grievously. [He] was quite eloquent in praise of Miss Isola. He says she is the most sensible girl and best female talker he knows; he wants to see her well married, great as the loss would be to him."

At the beginning of 1833, Moxon published *The Last Essays of Elia*, which proved to be Charles's final book. An earlier collection, *The First Essays of Elia* had appeared in volume form in 1823. Also, a pirated edition of that work had surfaced in the United States in 1828, where the sales had proved to be far healthier than those achieved in England.

At the end of May, Charles and Mary parted company with the Westwoods (whom Charles had grown to heartily dislike), and moved to Church Street, Edmonton. Doubtless there were some occasions when Charles found life as a lodger demeaning. Once, when visited by Wordsworth, 'Gaffer' Westwood noticed that the poet took what he regarded as an excessive amount of sugar in his tea. Charles was charged an extra sixpence for this perceived extravagance in his next week's bill; rather in the same way that less accommodating landladies of seaside boarding houses during the 1950s would charge their visitors a higher weekly tariff 'for the use of cruet' at mealtimes!

This would prove to be the last time that Charles and Mary moved house, and he explained the reasons for this latest upheaval in their domestic arrangements in a letter to Wordsworth, written at the time of their removal. "Mary is ill again. Her illnesses encroach yearly. The last was three months, followed by two of depression most dreadful. I look back upon her earlier attacks with longing; nice little durations of six weeks or so, followed by complete restoration, – shocking as they were to me then. In short, half her life she is dead to me, and the other half is made anxious with fears and lookings forward to the next shock. With such prospects, it seemed to me necessary that she should no longer live with me, and be fluttered with continual removals; so I am come to live with her, at a Mr. Walden's and his wife, who take in patients."

They were described in one recollection of them as making their living "by keeping in gentle restraint those whose attacks were harmless or intermittent, and whose friends looked for more humane treatment than was obtainable in the asylums of those days". The Waldens, Charles told Wordsworth, "have arranged to lodge and board us only. They have had the care of [Mary] before. I see little of her; alas! I too often hear her…

"To lay a little more load on it, a circumstance has happened… which, at another crisis, I should have more rejoiced in. I am about to lose my old and only walk-companion, whose mirthful spirits were the 'youth of our house', Emma Isola. I have her here now for a little while, but she is too nervous properly to be under such a roof, so she will make short visits – be no more an inmate. With my perfect approval, and more than concurrence, she is to be wedded to Moxon… Now to the brighter side. I am emancipated from the Westwoods, and I am with attentive people, and younger. I am three or four miles nearer the great city; coaches half-price less, and going always, of which I will avail myself. I have few friends left there, one or two though, most beloved. But London streets and faces cheer me inexpressibly… I am feeble, but cheerful in this my genial hot weather. Walked sixteen miles yesterday…".

On the 30th of July 1833, Moxon married Emma, and Charles gave her away. He wrote later that "in the role of grave father [I] behaved tolerably well… I tripped a little at the altar-piece, but, recalled seasonably by a Parsonic rebuke, 'Who gives this woman?', I was in time to reply resolutely, 'I do'.". Mary had been unable to attend the wedding owing to another bout of illness but, by the time Charles returned home from the ceremony, an almost unaccountable and sudden improvement had taken place in her condition. During the course of the wedding-day, Mrs. Walden had asked Mary's permission to drink a glass of wine as a toast to the newly married Moxons. "It restored me from that moment, as if by an electrical stroke, to the entire possession of my senses," she wrote to them later. "I never felt so calm and quiet after a similar illness as I do now. I feel as if all tears were wiped from my eyes, and all care from my heart." Charles added a brief postscript. "Never was such a calm or such a recovery. 'Tis her own words undictated." His sense of relief is palpable.

By now, Moxon had moved to the very fashionable address of Dover Street, Piccadilly and, as some measure of his success and of the esteem in which he was held by the literary fraternity, he was entrusted with publishing Wordsworth's poetry. In 1839, he issued the first complete edition of Shelley's poems, edited by the poet's wife Mary Shelley (best remembered, perhaps, as the author of *Frankenstein, or the Modern Prometheus* (1818). He died in 1858.

***

Charles spent his last birthday – his fifty-ninth – with the Moxons, but yet again Mary was ill and unable to join them. Charles wrote to Emma's old schoolfriend, Miss Fryer, on the 14th of February 1834: "When [Mary] is not violent, her rambling chat is better to me than the sense and sanity of this world. Her heart is obscured, not buried; it breaks out occasionally; and one can discern a strong mind struggling with the billows that have gone over it. I could be nowhere happier than under the same roof with her. Her memory is unnaturally strong; and from ages past, if we may so call the earliest records of our poor life, she fetches thousands of names and things that never would have dawned upon me again, and thousands from the ten years she lived before me. What took place from early girlhood to her coming of age principally lives again (every important thing, and every trifle) in her brain, with the vividness of real presence."

A very late glimpse of Charles and Mary out visiting friends together in London was provided by the young American poet, Nathaniel Parker Willis, who breakfasted with them at Crabb Robinson's rooms on the 19th of June 1834. "There was a rap at the door at last," wrote Willis, "and enter a gentleman in black small-clothes and gaiters, short and very slight in his person, his head set on his shoulders with a thoughtful, forward bent, his hair just sprinkled with gray [sic], a beautiful deep-set eye, aquiline nose, and a very indescribable mouth. Whether it expressed most humour or feeling, good-nature of a kind of whimsical peevishness, or twenty other things which passed over it by turns, I cannot in the least be certain.

"His sister, whose literary reputation is associated very closely with her brother's, and who as the original of 'Bridget Elia' is a kind of object for literary affection, came in after him. She is a small, bent figure, evidently a victim to ill-health, and hears with difficulty. Her face has been, I should think, a fine and handsome one, and her bright gray [sic] eye is still full of intelligence and fire. They both seemed quite at home in our friend's chambers; and as there was to be no one else, we immediately drew round the breakfast table… The conversation was very local. Our host and his guest had not met for some weeks, and they had a great deal to say of some mutual friends. Perhaps in this way, however, I saw more of the author, for his manner of speaking of them, and the quaint humour with which he complained of one, and spoke well of another, was so in the vein of his inimitable writings, that I could have fancied myself listening to an audible composition of new Elia. Nothing could be more delightful than the kindness and affection between the brother and his sister…

"Lamb ate nothing, and complained in a querulous tone of the veal pie… There was a kind of potted fish which he had expected our friend would procure for him. He enquired whether there was not a morsel left perhaps in the bottom of the last pot. Mr. R. was not sure. 'Send and see,' said Lamb, 'and if the pot has been cleaned send me the cover. I think the sight of it would do me good'… In the course of half an hour [the Lambs] took their leave… Wreck as he certainly is, and must be, however, of what he was, I would rather have seen him for that single hour, than the hundred-and-one sights of London put together."

During the following month, coming almost as a melancholy harbinger of his own fast-approaching death, Charles received the sad news that Coleridge, his dearest friend since their days together at Christ's Hospital, died on the 25th of July at Highgate, north London, where he had been living under medical supervision in the large family home of Dr. James Gillman. He was sixty-one. According to his biographer, Richard Holmes, in *Coleridge: Darker Reflections* (1998), "At 6.30a.m. he slipped into the dark. He was talking almost up to the end. As he closed those extraordinary eyes [he declared] that his mind was clear and 'quite unclouded'. Then he added with growing interest, 'I could even be witty…'."

Charles was deeply affected by Coleridge's death, and some months elapsed before he was able – in November – to set down his feelings on the matter. "When I heard of the death of Coleridge," he wrote, "it was without grief. It seemed to me that he long had been on the confines of the next world, – that he had a hunger for eternity. I grieved then that I could not grieve. But since, I feel how great a part he was of me. His great and dear spirit haunts me. I cannot think a thought, I cannot make a criticism on men and books, without an ineffectual turning and reference to him. He was the great proof and touchstone of all my cogitations… Great in his writings, he was the greatest in his conversation. In him was disproved that old maxim, that we should allow everyone his share of talk. He would talk from morn to dewy eve, nor cease till far midnight; yet whoever would interrupt him – who would obstruct that continuous flow of converse? …He had the tact of making the unintelligible seem plain… He was my fifty-years-old friend without a dissention. Never saw I his likeness, nor probably the world can see again. I seem to love the house he died at more passionately than when he lived. I love the faithful Gillmans more than while they exercised their virtues towards him living. What was his mansion is consecrated to me a chapel."

Charles and Coleridge met at best infrequently during their later years, but they were constantly – even if unconsciously – in each other's thoughts. In his will, Coleridge requested "that a small plain gold mourning ring, with my hair, be presented… to my close friend and ever-beloved schoolfellow, Charles Lamb – and in the deep and almost lifelong affection of which this is the slender record; his equally beloved sister, Mary Lamb, will know herself to be included".

Lucas notes that "the Lambs had been much in Coleridge's thoughts at the end. On his death-bed he had written, in pencil, in a copy of his *Poetical Works*, against the poem, *This Lime-Tree Bower my Prison*, the inscription: 'Ch. And Mary Lamb – dear to my heart, yea, as it were, my heart. S.T.C.'". The poem had been written thirty-seven years earlier, while Charles was staying at Nether Stowey during the summer following the great tragedy which had befallen his family.

***

On the morning of Monday the 22nd of December, Charles wrote to George Dyer's wife at Clifford's Inn, Holborn, "about a book which I either have lost or left at your house on Thursday. It was the book I went out to fetch… while the tripe was frying. I think I left it in the parlour. It is Mr. Cary's book, and I would not lose it for the world. Pray, if you find it, book it at the Swan, Snow Hill, by an Edmonton stage immediately, directed to Mr. Lamb, Church Street, Edmonton, or write to say you cannot find it. I am quite anxious about it. If it is lost, I shall never like tripe again!". Poignantly, this was the last letter he ever wrote. Later that same morning, he tripped on a stone while out walking and fell to the ground, cutting his cheek slightly in the accident. An infection developed and, with alarming speed, spread through his entire body. On the following Saturday morning, Charles's friend and executor, Thomas Talfourd, called on him at home "and found him very weak, and nearly insensible to things passing around him. Now and then a few words were audible, from which it seemed that his mind, in its feebleness, was intent on kind and hospitable thought… I do not think he knew me; and having vainly tried to gain his attention, I quitted him, not believing his death so near at hand. In less than an hour afterwards, his voice gradually grew fainter, as he still murmured the names of Moxon, Procter, and some other old friends and he sank into death as placidly as into sleep". He died on the 27th of December, 1834, aged fifty-nine.

Mary, wrote Lucas, "was at once visited by an attack of her malady that mercifully deprived her of any true sense of what was happening". A few days later, on New Year's Day 1835, Crabb Robinson wrote that he had "received a letter from Talfourd, informing him that Miss Lamb is quite insane, yet conscious of her brother's death without feeling it [a similar response to that which she evinced towards the death of her mother] and able to point out the place for the grave". Charles was buried in the churchyard at Edmonton and, in May 1847, at the venerable age of eighty-two, Mary was reunited with him there in death. She had spent the last six years of her life under the care of a nurse at St. John's Wood in northwest London, "for the most part in the shadow but occasionally her old self", as Lucas movingly expressed it.

The house where Charles ended his days is now called Lamb's Cottage. It is enticingly tucked away at the end of a long and narrow garden path, incongruously secluded in the heart of today's crowded and busily urban Edmonton. It is not open to the public but, having kindly been given access on my own brief visit there, I know it is possible to feel that his spirit hovers over the place still.

***

Coleridge, writing in an article that appeared posthumously in the *Monthly Repository* in 1835, described Charles as having "more totality and individuality of character than any other man I know, or have ever known in all my life. In most men we distinguish between the different powers of their intellect as one being predominant over the other. The genius of Wordsworth is greater than his talent, tho' considerable. The talent of Southey is greater than his genius, though respectable; and so on. But in Charles Lamb it is altogether one; his genius is talent and his talent is genius, and his heart is as whole and one as his head".

George Dyer, writing in the *Gentleman's Magazine* during the same year, said of Charles that "his faculties were extraordinary. The wit that he brought with him from school continued to flow uniformly and to increase through the whole course of his life. It was almost as natural with him to say witty things as to breathe; he could not enter a room without a joke, and he may be said to have almost conversed in extemporaneous humour. Nor did his discourse consist of merely sportive pleasantries; they had often the force of eloquence joined with the solidity of argument, enlivened and softened by a humanity and benevolence which invariably beamed in his countenance".

Moxon wrote of his father-in-law (again in 1835), that "he was an admirable critic, and was always willing to exercise the art he so much excelled in for the fame of others. We have seen him almost blind with poring over the endless and illegible manuscripts that were submitted to him. On these occasions, how he would long to find out something good, something that he could speak kindly of, for to give another pain was to give himself greater.

"His tastes, in many respects, were most singular. He preferred Wardour Street and Seven Dials to fields that were Elysian. The disappearance of the old clock from St. Dunstan's Church drew tears from him; nor could he ever pass without emotion the place where Exeter 'Change once stood... The Garden of Eden, he used to say, must have been a dull place. He had a strong aversion to roast beef and to fowls, and to any wines but port and sherry. Tripe and cow-heel were to him delicacies – rare dainties! He could not pack up a trunk, nor tie up a parcel. Yet he was methodical, punctual in his appointments, and an excellent pay-master. A debt haunted him."

Hine wrote, in 1949, that "Elia was a law unto himself. No one ever wrote like him before; no one has succeeded in writing like him since". However, perhaps it is Lucas who has provided the near-perfect summation. "The life of Charles Lamb," he wrote, "is the narrative of one who was a man and brother first, an East India clerk next, and a writer afterwards... The story is that rather of a private individual who chanced to have literary genius than a man of letters in the ordinary sense of the term. The work of Charles Lamb forms no integral part of the history of English Literature: he is not in the main current, he is hardly in the side current of the great stream. As that noble river flows steadily onward it brims here and there into a clear and peaceful bay. Of such tributary backwaters, which are of the stream yet not in it, Charles Lamb [is one]."

Afterword

The poet and essayist, Walter Savage Landor, was just eleven days older than Charles, and visited him at Enfield in September 1832. It was the only occasion on which the two men met. "The world will never see again two such delightful volumes as *The Essays of Elia*," wrote Landor. "No man living is capable of writing the worst twenty pages of them." He subsequently composed the following verse tribute:

> *Once, and once only, have I seen thy face,*
> *Elia! Only once has thy tripping tongue*
> *Run o'er my breast, yet never has been left*
> *Impression on it stronger or more sweet.*
> *Cordial old man! What youth was in thy years,*
> *What wisdom in thy levity, what truth*
> *In every utterance of that purest soul!*
> *Few are the spirits of the glorified*
> *I'd spring to earlier at the gate of Heaven.*

Bibliography

Ackroyd, Peter, London: The Biography, Chatto & Windus 2000.
Ainger, Alfred, The Letters of Charles Lamb, vols. 1 & 2, Macmillan & Co. 1891.
Bellot, Hugh H. L., The Inner and Middle Temple: Legal, Literary and Historic Associations, Methuen & Co. 1902.
Cecil, David, A Portrait of Charles Lamb, Constable & Company Limited 1983.
Christ's Hospital Book, Hamish Hamilton 1953.
De Quincey, Thomas, Recollections of Charles Lamb, Tait's Edinburgh Magazine 1838.
Francis, Basil, Fanny Kelly of Drury Lane, Rockliff Publishing Corporation Ltd. 1950.
Hanff, Helene, 84 Charing Cross Road, Andre Deutsch Ltd. 1971.
Hankinson, Alan, Coleridge Walks the Fells, Ellenbank Press 1991.
Hine, Reginald, Charles Lamb and his Hertfordshire, J.M. Dent & Sons Ltd. 1949.
Hood, Thomas, Hood's Own (Second Series), E. Moxon, Son & Co. undated.
Jerrold, Walter, Thomas Hood & Charles Lamb, The Story of a

Friendship, Ernest Benn Ltd. 1930.
Johnson, Edith Christina, Lamb Always Elia, Methuen & Co. Ltd. 1935.
Jones, Stanley, Life of Hazlitt, Oxford University Press, 1989.
Lamb, Charles, The Essays of Elia, and The Last Essays of Elia, Walter Scott Ltd. 1890.
Lamb, Charles and Mary, Mrs. Leicester's School, 1809.
Lamb, Charles and Mary, Tales from Shakespeare, 1807.
Lucas, E.V., A Life of Charles Lamb (2 Vols.), Methuen & Co., 1905.
Martin, Benjamin Ellis, In the Footprints of Charles Lamb, Richard Bentley and Son, 1891.
Morpurgo, J.E., (Ed.), The Autobiography of Leigh Hunt, 1850, The Cresset Press Ltd. 1948 ed.
Proctor, Bryan Waller, ('Barry Cornwall'), Charles Lamb: A Memoir, 1866.
Shaffer, Mary Ann & Barrow, Annie, The Guernsey Literary and Potato Peel Pie Society, Bloomsbury Publishing plc. 2008.
Talfourd, Thomas, Charles Lamb: Final Memorials, Edward Moxon, 1850.
Thomas, Edward, A Literary Pilgrim in England, Oxford University Press, 1980 ed.

Index of People and Places

Ackroyd, Peter, 2, 3, 63
Ainger, Canon Alfred, 87
Alfoxden, (Somerset), 62, 63

Bacon, Francis, 45
Balmanno, Mrs., 155
Barbauld, Mrs., 78
Barrow, Annie, xiv
Barton, Bernard, 125, 130,140, 141, 147,158, 168, 169
Bath, (Somerset), 81, 84, 107, 116
Belcher, Muriel, 45
Bellot, Hugh H.L., 3
Bird, William, 20-22, 29
Blakesware, (Herts.), 9-12, 41, 65, 88, 104, 163
Blenheims, (Herts.), 41, 47, 163, 164
Boswell, James,5, 20, 133
Bristol, (Avon), 45, 49, 64, 107
Bruton, Mary, 9
Burney, Captain, 92
Burney, Fanny, 92
Burney, Martin, 92,157
Button Snap, (Cherry Green, Herts.), 98-101

Calne, (Wilts.), 107
Cambridge, 68, 105, 106
    Jesus College, 43
    King's College, 105
    St. John's College, 105
    Trinity College,105
    Trumpington Street, 106, 148
Carlyle, Thomas, 172-174
Cecil, Lord David, 51, 164
Cherry Green, (Herts.), (see Button Snap),
Chippenham, (Wilts.), 107
Clare, John, 129
Clarke, Charles Cowden, 159, 160
Clarke, Mary, 159
Coe, Mrs., (formerly Elizabeth Hunt), 162

Coleridge, Samuel Taylor, 15, passim
Coleridge, Sara, 61
Colony Room Club, (Soho), 45
Congreve, William, 5
Cottle, Joseph, 64
Coventry, Thomas, 36, 37
Cowley, Abraham, 10, 87
Cowper, William, 5

'Dash', (Thomas Hood's dog), 143, 152, 153
DeQuincey, Thomas, 82-84
Dickens, Charles, 2, 59
Dove Cottage, (Grasmere), 80
Dyer, George, 77, 93, 135, 136, 181, 183

Elizabeth 1st, 3
Enfield, (formerly Middx.), 19, 71, 143, 144, 151, 153, 154, 157-161, 165, 167, 168, 170, 171, 174, 175
    Chase Side, 143, 144, 146, 151, 156, 159
    Southgate, 160
    Winchmore Hill, 160
Evelyn, John, 5, 143

Field, Edward, 9
Field, Mary, 9-11, 41, 164
Fielde, Francis, 4, 12, 13, 98, 99

Fielding, Henry, 5
Fornham, (Suffolk), 149, 168
France, 128
    Amiens, 129
    Dieppe, 128
    Paris, 128-130
    Sienne, River, 129
Francis, Basil, xiv, 116, 120, 157

Garrick, David, 12, 13, 147
Goddard House School, (Widford), 161, 162
Godwin, William, 77, 82, 85, 92, 97, 100, 123
Goldsmith, Oliver, 5
Gordon, Lord George, 20
Greta Hall, (Keswick), 78, 79
Gutch, John Matthew, 72-74

Hanff, Helene, xiv
Hankinson, Alan, 46
Hatton, Christopher, 4
Hazlitt, William, 81, 82, 86, 93-97, 100, 101, 117, 152, 156, 170
Helvellyn, (Cumbria), 80
Hertford, (Herts.), 24, 25
Hetty, Aunt, 16, 28, 51, 52, 57-60, 67
Hine, Reginald, 11, 98, 99, 100, 104, 163, 184
Hitchin, (Herts.), 9
Holmes, Richard, 79, 180

Index of People and Places

Hood, Thomas, 19, 131-134, 143, 152-156
Horsham, (West Sussex), 24, 25
Hunt, (James) Leigh, 22, 23, 27, 34, 75, 97, 114, 116, 117, 134, 136, 137, 144, 156
Hutchinson, Sara, 104, 107, 108

Irving, Washington, 2
Isola, Charles, 148, 149
Isola, Emma, 147-150, 157-159, 168, 169, 176-178

Jerrold, Walter, 132
Johnson, Samuel, 5, 20, 32, 44, 133

Keats, John, 133, 160
Kelly, Frances, (Fanny), xiv, 114-121, 155-157
Kelly, Michael, 114
Keswick, (Cumbria), (also see Greta Hall), 99
King's Walden, (Herts.), 9

Lamb, Charles, xiii, passim
Lamb, Elizabeth, (mother), 8, 12, 15, 16, 42, 49, 51, 54, 57
Lamb, John, (father), 6, 7, 12, 16, 42, 51, 57-59, 66, 67
Lamb, John, (brother), 6, 14, 15, 17, 38, 43, 58, 85, 92, 143
Lamb, Mary Anne, (sister), xiii, passim
Lamb, Sarah, (see Hetty, Aunt),

Landor, Walter Savage, 186
LeGrice, Charles Valentine, 29
Leishman, Mrs., 143, 151
Lincoln, (Lincs.), 8
Lloyd, Charles, 61
London,
    Adelphi, 155
    Bethlem, ('Bedlam'), 52
    Charterhouse, 25
    Christ's Hospital, ('Blue-coat School'), 22-25, 27-37, 43, 44, 72, 128, 135, 180
    City of London, xiii, 5, 31, 38
    Clerkenwell, 67
    Clifford's Inn, (Holborn), 136, 181
    Colebrooke Cottage, (Islington), 130-134, 144, 150-153
    Covent Garden, 71, 110, 122, 130, 134, 149
    Crown Office Row, (Temple), 4, 5, 16, 43
    Dalston, 107, 108
    Drury Lane Theatre, 12, 14, 76, 78, 84, 110, 115, 116
    East India House, xiii, 26, 41-43, 48, 57, 78, 82, 84, 101, 107, 111, 139, 142

Edmonton, (Church Street), 176, 182, 183
Embankment, The, 1, 5
Fetter Lane, 21, 22, 105, 106
Fitzroy Street, 164
Fleet Street, 1, 2, 36, 81, 93
Fountain Court, (Temple), 2, 5
Gray's Inn, 3
Hackney, 62, 107
Hare Court, (Temple), 90, 91, 108
Hoxton Asylum, 48, 50, 68
Inner Temple Lane, 90-92, 116
Islington, 19, 52, 59, 130, 134, 139, 146, 153, 154
King's Bench Walk, (Temple), 74, 75
Leadenhall Street, 41, 82, 101, 107, 113
Leicester Square, 164
Lincoln's Inn, 3
Lincoln's Inn Fields, 45
Little Queen Street, (Holborn), 43, 49, 51, 57, 59
Lyceum, The, 114, 116, 120
Middle Temple, 3
Mitre Court Buildings, (Temple), 74, 75, 84, 89-91
Newgate Street, 23, 24, 43
New River, The, 31, 130, 135
Pentonville, 59, 68, 70, 72, 74
Russell Street, (Covent Garden), 110, 116, 122, 130, 134, 148
Salutation and Cat, The, 43-45, 55
Soho, 45, 170
Southampton Buildings, (Holborn), 68, 73, 74, 90, 101, 170
South-Sea House, 38, 39, 41, 92, 124, 128
Strand, The, 2, 81, 114, 121
Temple Church, 4
Thames, River, 5, 74, 129

Lucas, E.V., 6, 13, 19, 36, 40, 41, 47, 55, 66, 87, 88, 94, 96, 114, 119, 120, 126, 139, 146, 147, 162, 164, 173, 174, 181-184

Macaulay, Thomas Babington, 100
Mackery End, (Herts.), 9, 88, 102-104

Manning, Thomas, 68, 72, 74, 79-81, 84, 89, 90
Marlborough, (Wilts.), 107
Martin, B.E., 5, 17, 28, 45, 49, 70, 91 142
Maseres, Baron, 74
Montagu, Basil, 97
Moxon, Edward, 149, 150, 154, 169-171, 174, 176-178, 182, 184
Murry, John Middleton, 33

Nether Stowey, (Somerset), 61-65, 77, 181
Norris, Randal, 51, 161

Ollier, James, 111

Paice, Joseph, 37, 38, 42
Patmore, P.G., 152, 153
Penrith, (Cumbria), 79, 99
Penton, Harry, 59
Plumer family, 9, 11, 12
Ponders End, (formerly Middx.), 138
Poole, Thomas, 27, 65
Potters Bar, (Herts.), 71
Proctor, Bryan Waller, ('Barry Cornwall'), 68, 121, 122, 123, 143, 182

Racedown Lodge, (Dorset), 62
Reynolds, Mrs, 19, 20, 29

Richardson, Samuel, 44
Robinson, Henry Crabb, 92, 121, 128, 129, 143, 161, 171, 175, 179, 182
Rogers, Samuel, 169

Salisbury, (Wilts.), 96, 97
Salt, Samuel, 6-8, 12, 14, 18, 25, 32, 36, 42, 49, 67, 88, 96, 158
Shaffer, Mary Ann, xiv
Shakespeare, William, 3, 32, 36, 85-87, 94, 126, 160
Shelley, Mary, 178
Shelley, Percy Bysshe, 133, 134, 178
Sheridan, Richard Brinsley, 12, 13, 115
Siddons, Mrs., 12, 55, 56
Simmons, Ann, 41, 47, 48, 55, 163, 164
Skiddaw, (Cumbria), 74, 80, 81
Southey, Robert, 10, 43, 45-47, 64, 67, 78, 113, 122, 144, 146, 170, 171, 183
Spenser, Edmund, 5
Stamford, (Lincs.), 6
Stoddart, Sarah, (later Mrs. Hazlitt), 86, 95, 96, 135
Swindlestock Tavern, (Oxford), 4

Talfourd, Thomas, 92, 182
Thomas, Edward, 104

Walden, Mr. & Mrs., 177, 178
Walton, Izaak, 8, 71, 138

Westmill, (Herts.), 98, 100
Westwood, 'Gaffer', 151, 165, 167, 171, 176, 177
Westwood, Thomas, 151, 155-157
Wheathampstead, (Herts.), 9, 104
Widford, (Herts.), (see also Goddard House School), 9, 11, 65, 161-164
Williams, Mrs., 149, 168
Willis, Nathaniel Parker, 179
Wilson, John, ('Christopher North'), 174, 175
Winterslow, (Wilts.), 95-97
Wordsworth, Dorothy, 62, 63, 65, 77, 78, 80, 84, 108, 121, 143, 167
Wordsworth, William, 33, 62, 63, 65, 77, 78, 80, 82, 85, 86, 93, 104, 106, 113, 117, 121, 133, 138, 140, 141, 147-149, 157, 165, 176-178, 183
Wren, Sir Christopher, 44